W9-BTS-120

**Taiga**

Chelsea House
An imprint of Infobase Publishing
132 West 31st Street
New York NY 10001

**Library of Congress Cataloging-in-Publication Data**
Day, Trevor.
Taiga / Trevor Day ; illustrations by Richard Garratt.
   p. cm.—(Biomes of the Earth)
  Includes bibliographical references and index.
  ISBN 0-8160-5329-4
  1. Taigas—Juvenile literature. I. Title. II. Series.
  QH86.D39 2006
  577.3'7—dc22                                        2005009791

Chelsea House books are available at special discounts when purchased in bulk quantities for businesses, associations, institutions, or sales promotions. Please call our Special Sales Department in New York at (212) 967-8800 or (800) 322-8755.

You can find Chelsea House on the World Wide Web at http://www.chelseahouse.com

Text design by David Strelecky
Cover design by Cathy Rincon
Illustrations by Richard Garratt
Photo research by Elizabeth H. Oakes

Printed in China

CP Hermitage 10 9 8 7 6 5 4 3 2 1

This book is printed on acid-free paper.

*From Richard Garratt:*
*To Chantal, who has lightened my darkness*

# CONTENTS

# PREFACE

Earth is a remarkable planet. There is nowhere else in our solar system where life can survive in such a great diversity of forms. As far as we can currently tell, our planet is unique. Isolated in the barren emptiness of space, here on Earth we are surrounded by a remarkable range of living things, from the bacteria that inhabit the soil to the great whales that migrate through the oceans, from the giant redwood trees of the Pacific forests to the mosses that grow on urban sidewalks. In a desolate universe, Earth teems with life in a bewildering variety of forms.

One of the most exciting things about the Earth is the rich pattern of plant and animal communities that exists over its surface. The hot, wet conditions of the equatorial regions support dense rain forests with tall canopies occupied by a wealth of animals, some of which may never touch the ground. The cold, bleak conditions of the polar regions, on the other hand, sustain a much lower variety of species of plants and animals, but those that do survive under such harsh conditions have remarkable adaptations to their testing environment. Between these two extremes lie many other types of complex communities, each well suited to the particular conditions of climate prevailing in its region. Scientists call these communities *biomes*.

The different biomes of the world have much in common with one another. Each has a plant component, which is responsible for trapping the energy of the Sun and making it available to the other members of the community. Each has grazing animals, both large and small, that take advantage of the store of energy found within the bodies of plants. Then come the predators, ranging from tiny spiders that feed upon even smaller insects to tigers, eagles, and polar bears that survive by preying upon large animals. All of these living things form a complicated network of feeding interactions, and, at the base of the system, microbes in the soil are ready to consume the energy-rich plant litter or dead animal flesh that remains. The biome, then, is an integrated unit within which each species plays its particular role.

This set of books aims to outline the main features of each of the Earth's major biomes. The biomes covered include the tundra habitats of polar regions and high mountains, the taiga (boreal forest) and temperate forests of somewhat warmer lands, the grasslands of the prairies and the tropical savanna, the deserts of the world's most arid locations, and the tropical forests of the equatorial regions. The wetlands of the world, together with river and lake habitats, do not lie neatly in climatic zones over the surface of the Earth but are scattered over the land. And the oceans are an exception to every rule. Massive in their extent, they form an interconnecting body of water extending down into unexplored depths, gently moved by global currents.

Humans have had an immense impact on the environment of the Earth over the past 10,000 years since the last Ice Age. There is no biome that remains unaffected by the presence of the human species. Indeed, we have created our own biome in the form of agricultural and urban lands, where people dwell in greatest densities. The farms and cities of the Earth have their own distinctive climates and natural history, so they can be regarded as a kind of artificial biome that people have created, and they are considered as a separate biome in this set.

Each biome is the subject of a separate volume. Each richly illustrated book describes the global distribution, the climate, the rocks and soils, the plants and animals, the history, and the environmental problems found within each biome. Together, the set provides students with a sound basis for understanding the wealth of the Earth's biodiversity, the factors that influence it, and the future dangers that face the planet and our species.

Is there any practical value in studying the biomes of the Earth? Perhaps the most compelling reason to understand the way in which biomes function is to enable us to conserve their rich biological resources. The world's productivity is the basis of the human food supply. The world's biodiversity holds a wealth of unknown treasures, sources of drugs and medicines that will help to improve the quality of life. Above all, the world's biomes are a constant source of wonder, excitement, recreation, and inspiration that feed not only our bodies but also our minds and spirits. These books aim to provide the information about biomes that readers need in order to understand their function, draw upon their resources, and, most of all, enjoy their diversity.

# ACKNOWLEDGMENTS

I would like to thank the team that helped create this book: illustrator Richard Garratt, picture researcher Elizabeth Oakes, project editor Dorothy Cummings, and executive editor Frank Darmstadt, who commissioned and managed the project. A final thank you to my partner Christina, who is unswerving in encouraging me and my work.

# INTRODUCTION

A biome is a major ecological zone on Earth's surface. Scientists normally define a biome by the community of plants within it. The plants, in turn, dictate which kinds of animals live there. The plant community reflects the nature of the soil conditions and the prevailing climate. Hot deserts contain plants and animals that are adapted to high temperatures and scarcity of water. Tropical rain forest organisms, on the other hand, thrive at similar temperatures but where rainfall is much higher. Boreal forest, or taiga, the subject of this book, is the biome defined by its northerly distribution and its abundance of conifer trees (trees with needles instead of broad leaves and cones instead of flowers).

Most biologists recognize about 10 biomes, all but one of which are found on land. The biomes include taiga or boreal forest (northern forests of conifer trees), temperate forest (hardwoods, or mixed forests of hardwoods and conifers), tropical rain forest, tropical seasonal forest, desert, alpine (mountains), grassland, wetland, and tundra. The ocean biome is unlike all the others. It spans all climates, from icy polar waters to warm tropical seas.

Chapter 1 of this book explores the geography of the taiga. It explains what taiga is, where it is found, and why it is found there. It describes typical taiga landscapes and then considers the world's four taiga regions: North American, European, Siberian, and Far Eastern.

Chapter 2 reveals the geology of the taiga. It explains how the bedrock beneath the Canadian taiga has been shaped by the movement of Earth's plates and then sculpted by glaciers. The chapter describes taiga soils and permafrost (permanently frozen ground) and its influence on soil structure and plant life.

Chapter 3 considers taiga's weather and climate. The Earth's changing climate influences the nature and distribution of the taiga. Human activities appear to be accelerating global climate change.

As chapter 4 explains, the assemblage of animals and plants that thrive in the taiga is smaller—in variety and abundance—than in most other biomes. Chapter 5 considers ecological processes that govern the lives of taiga's organisms.

Chapter 6 chronicles the origins of taiga's peoples and reveals how they have adapted to the unique set of conditions in the boreal forest. Their experience provides some insight into how and why the taiga should be valued.

As chapter 7 also makes clear, the taiga provides many products and services, some of which are taken entirely for granted by people living outside the biome. Traditional taiga lifestyles based on hunting, fishing, and gathering have been joined by the working practices of modern forestry, agriculture, and mining industries. These industries are powered, in some cases, by electricity from hydroelectric systems. Today, traditional and modern methods for exploiting taiga's resources often exist side by side in a mixed economy.

The activities of people have removed or altered much of the world's taiga, and they continue to do so today. As chapter 8 explains, people have depleted many of taiga's animal populations through overhunting and overfishing. Clearcutting of forests, followed by changes in land use, has substantially altered the area of taiga in the last 2,000 years. Those large forests that remain are becoming increasingly fragmented. Human activities have altered the boreal forest by introducing foreign species of plant and animal, creating air and water pollution, and flooding the land. Most pervasive of all are the effects of human-induced climate change.

To manage the taiga effectively, we first need to know what is there. The last chapter explains how modern survey methods, ranging from remote sensing from a satellite or aircraft to monitoring the age and health of individual trees, are revolutionizing our understanding of the taiga. A range of strategies, from forest regeneration and the controlled use of fire to creating protected areas and conserving genetic diversity, seeks to manage the taiga in a sustainable manner. The taiga has a key role to play in climate warming, a process that is changing the nature and distribution of the world's northern forests. If we are to conserve the taiga, then we need to understand how its biological processes work and manage these northern forests with a lighter and wiser touch than we do at present.

The two greatest expanses of taiga lie in Canada and Russia. More examples are provided from the Canadian experience because, for the moment, the quantity and quality of their readily available information, and its ease of interpretation, is generally greater.

# CHAPTER 1

# GEOGRAPHY OF THE TAIGA

The chilling, distant howl of a wolf, the staccato hammering of a woodpecker nearby, the bounce of the dense carpet of conifer needles underfoot. The shaft of pure light slicing through the canopy of tall, dark, brooding trees. The crisp air rich with resinous fragrance. These are some of the sensory impressions any visitor to the great north woods can experience. This is the taiga.

## What is taiga?

The word *taiga* originates from northern Russia, where it was originally used to describe the dense woodlands of spruce—a type of conifer tree—found in cool, wet climates. In the 20th century, the term came to include all cool, northern coniferous forests, including the so-called boreal forests of North America and Europe (from the Latin *Boreas,* the god of the north wind). Some researchers also refer to the coniferous forest of the mountains of warm temperate regions as taiga. Some of these mountain forests, such as those of the Alps in Europe and the Appalachians and the southern Rockies in the United States, are mentioned in this volume but are described more fully in other volumes in the series.

Climatic conditions in the taiga environment are cool and wet. The winters tend to be long and severe, with up to six months of the year having average daily temperatures below freezing. The summers are short, often with fewer than 100 frost-free days, and this produces a characteristically short growing season. A growing season of about three months or less distinguishes taiga from other types of lowland, coniferous forest found in more southerly latitudes of the Northern Hemisphere, such as the pine forests of Italy and Spain,

1

where temperatures are warmer and the growing season longer. In the Southern Hemisphere, there are also forests of conifers (albeit very different species), but these, too, are found in warmer climates. In the Southern Hemisphere, in the latitudes where taiga might be found—between about 45° and 70° latitude—the Earth's surface is mostly covered by ocean. Hence, there is no comparable forest to taiga in the Southern Hemisphere.

Conifer trees dominate the taiga. They are members of the group of seed-bearing plants that belong to the class Gymnospermae (meaning "naked seeds"), the *gymnosperms*. They have needlelike leaves and bear cones instead of flowers. Most of taiga's conifers belong to four groups: spruces (genus *Picea*), firs (*Abies*), pines (*Pinus*), and larches, or tamaracks (*Larix*). All except the larches are evergreen (they keep most of their leaves year-round). Larches are deciduous—they periodically shed their leaves, usually in winter.

## Where is taiga?

According to some biologists, taiga covers about 11 percent of the Earth's land surface, an area similar to that occupied by hot desert and arguably larger than that covered by tropical rain forest. Experts do not agree on the precise extent of the world's biomes because they use different criteria to identify the exact borders of each.

*The beauty of the taiga. Dense conifer forest surrounding a lake in Denali National Park, Alaska. Subtle differences in soil type and climate produce variations in the sizes and types of trees found between the edge of the lake in the foreground and the base of the mountains in the distance.* (Courtesy of Tom Mangelsen/ Minden Pictures)

pointed apex

conical arrangement of branches

cones and
needlelike leaves

straight trunk with lower section
devoid of branches

*The typical features of a
conifer tree*

The main lowland zone of taiga lies between latitudes of about 70°N and 45°N at its extremes, with most of the biome situated between about 60°N and 50°N. Taiga forms an almost continuous belt of forest across landmasses, from the Pacific coast of Canada and the United States in the west to the Pacific shores of Siberia and as far east as Kamchatka and northern Japan. This belt is interrupted in northwest Europe, where the North Atlantic Drift warms the climate and true taiga is more localized. Over many hundreds of years, people clearing the forest for fuel and to create space for agricultural crops or livestock farming have removed most of the taiga in Scotland and parts of Scandinavia.

Taiga is bordered to the north by tundra—treeless plains of moss, lichen, heather, dwarf shrubs, and tough grasses.

# Why conifers?

Why are conifers the dominant trees of the taiga? The answer lies in the handful of adaptations that enable conifers to cope with the cold, the snow, and the lack of available water. Although water is abundant throughout the year, for many months it is locked in ice.

- Most conifers are conical in overall shape, with their branches angled slightly downward. Snow, rather than settling on the leaves and snapping branches, tends to slide off.
- The needle leaves have a thick, waxy coating and a small area of surface. This reduces their tendency to lose water by evaporation. This is particularly important in winter, when the ground is frozen and the trees cannot replenish water they lose by taking in fresh supplies through their roots.
- Most conifers are evergreens. This means they can use their leaves to photosynthesize (make food using trapped sunlight energy) as soon as temperatures warm. Unlike deciduous trees, they do not have to wait to grow a new set of leaves at the start of the short growing season before they can photosynthesize.

Here, temperatures rise above 50°F (10°C) for only a few weeks in the year, and the available sunlight supports only a short growing season—too short for full-size trees to grow.

The taiga-tundra boundary is a transitional zone, called an *ecotone,* where treeless tundra gives way only gradually to dense, coniferous forest. Here, clumps of trees are interspersed by patches of tundra. Where sheltered valleys extend into the tundra, conifers hug the valley sides. Within the taiga, where the ground is too damp or too cold and wind-exposed to support tree growth, tundra-like conditions exist in isolated pockets.

The southern border of the taiga, like its northern counterpart, is an ecotone. Moving south from dense taiga, conifer-dominated forest gradually gives way to mixed conifer and broad-leaved forest, to almost pure broad-leaved forest, or to temperate grassland.

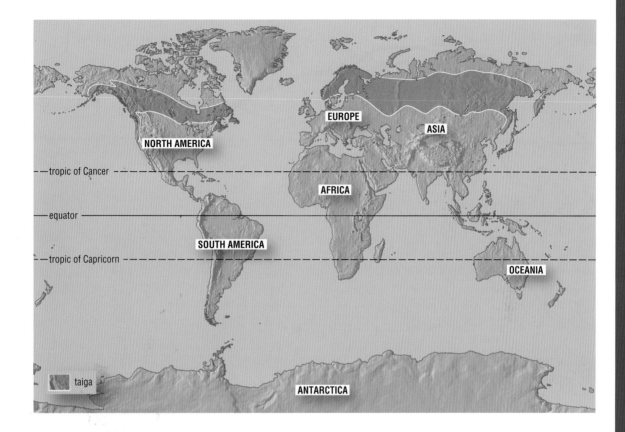

*The global distribution of taiga*

## Taiga landscapes

Compared with that of the temperate, broad-leaved woodland lying just south of the taiga, the diversity of life in conifer forests is small. Vast areas of taiga are dominated by one or two species of conifer. In the Canadian Shield region of eastern Canada, for example, the black spruce (*Picea mariana*) dominates thousands of square miles of landscape with thin soils. In eastern Siberia, the Daurian larch (*Larix gmelinii*) is widely distributed, from uplands to lowlands, and from taiga's northern to its southern border. In many places, the larch is the dominant large conifer (see the sidebar "Harsh survivors," page 6).

Two factors help account for the low biological diversity. The harsh conditions, particularly the long, bitterly cold winters with little water available for plants to use, limit the number of tree species to only the most hardy. Second, large tracts of taiga forest are comparatively new, having advanced

## Dark and light taiga

Viewed from an aircraft or balloon, the taiga forest landscape below is a patchwork of green hues. Where spruces and firs dominate, their dark green leaves create expanses of *dark taiga*. Larches and pine trees with paler green leaves produce so-called *light taiga*.

northward since the thaw at the end of the last major ice age some 15,000 years ago. This window of opportunity is probably too brief for new tree species to evolve.

Nevertheless, the taiga is far from being a monotonous blanket of trees. Subtle differences in climate and soil drainage create changes in vegetation cover even in the dense heart of taiga country. In Alaska and Canada, for example, black spruce colonizes the hollows in north-facing slopes. These trees can withstand the cold, damp conditions, the almost waterlogged soil, and the lack of nutrients. White spruce (*Picea glauca*) and birches (genus *Betula*) prefer warmer, drier, south-facing slopes that do not have a deep frozen layer (permafrost). Jack pines (*Pinus banksiana*) favor drier, warmer sites at higher altitudes and thrive where fires regularly burn back the vegetation. Willow (genus *Salix*), birch, and alder (genus *Alnus*) trees grow in

## Harsh survivors

Among taiga trees, larches survive the toughest conditions of all. Unlike other conifers, they shed their leaves in winter. Doing so, they reduce water loss and help prevent frost damage. Their roots cannot penetrate far down because of the deeply frozen ground (permafrost), but they are spread over a wide area to capture any available moisture. The roots also provide a firm anchor to withstand winter gales and frost heave—when frozen ground expands and lifts the surface soil.

damp ground close to bogs, lakes, and rivers. These are broad-leaved trees belonging to the group of seed-bearing plants called *angiosperms* (class Angiospermae), meaning "enclosed seeds." Distinct from conifers, such trees have broad, flat leaves supported by veins, as opposed to the needle leaves of conifers. Angiosperms also differ from conifers in producing flowers as reproductive structures, rather than cones, and their seeds are enclosed in fruit.

## North American taiga

Taiga is the dominant type of forest in Alaska and the whole of mainland Canada. In North America, the taiga extends in a wide, green belt from Alaska in the west to Newfoundland in the east. It borders the tundra to the north and touches the Great Lakes to the south. As in other boreal forests of the world, conifers are the dominant types of tree. They are well adapted to cope with thin, nutrient-poor soils and withstand long, harsh winters.

*Giant trunks of Douglas fir (Pseudotsuga menziesii) in an old-growth forest on Vancouver Island, British Columbia, Canada. These firs, with their deeply fissured bark, are among the world's tallest trees. Notice the lush growth of ferns on the ground and moss on the lower tree trunks. This is indicative of a warmer climate than is found in most of the taiga.* (Courtesy of Gerry Ellis/ Minden Pictures)

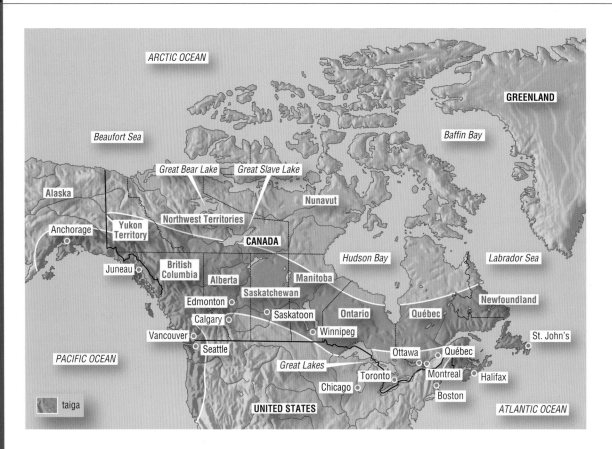

ARCTIC OCEAN

GREENLAND

Beaufort Sea

Baffin Bay

Great Bear Lake    Great Slave Lake

Alaska

Nunavut

Anchorage

Yukon
Territory

Northwest Territories

CANADA

Hudson Bay

Labrador Sea

Juneau

British
Columbia

Alberta

Manitoba

Newfoundland

Edmonton

Saskatchewan

Calgary

Saskatoon

Ontario

Québec

St. John's

Vancouver

Winnipeg

PACIFIC OCEAN

Seattle

Ottawa    Québec

Great Lakes

Toronto

Montreal    Halifax

Chicago

Boston

taiga

UNITED STATES

ATLANTIC OCEAN

*The distribution of taiga
in North America*

Biologists describe three broad bands of American taiga extending from north to south. In the north lies open taiga forest with scattered spruces, American larches (*Larix laricina*), and lichens. Moving south, the taiga gradually becomes dense forest with the addition of pine trees, firs (genus *Abies*), aspens (genus *Populus*), and birches. To the southeast, in southern Ontario, Quebec, and the Maritime Provinces of New Brunswick, Prince Edward Island, and Nova Scotia, the dense taiga gives way to an ecotone consisting of conifers such as white pine (*Pinus strobus*) mixed with broad-leaved trees that include sugar maple (*Acer saccharum*) and American beech (*Fagus grandifolia*).

Moving south from the lowland taiga belt of North America, low-altitude temperatures become too warm to sustain true taiga. However, at higher altitudes (high above sea level) suitable conditions for taiga-like growth exist on mountain slopes, where temperatures are cooler. Therefore, trees typical of the taiga are found at increasingly higher altitudes moving south. Near the northern end of North America's Rocky Mountains, the cold conditions limit the growth of conifer forests to an altitude of only 4,900 feet (1,500 m), known as the timberline. More than 1,300 miles (2,100 km) to the south, in and around Colorado, the Rockies are bathed in a warmer climate. Here, the belt of conifer forest only begins at about 6,900 feet (2,130 m) above sea level. The timberline reaches an altitude of about 9,800 feet (3,000 m).

Throughout the North American taiga, the edges of bogs (muskegs) support dark conifers, especially black spruce. Lakes and rivers divide the taiga landscape into a patchwork. Canada has more lakes than any other country of comparable size, and most of these are located within the taiga zone.

More than 200 species of birds nest in the North American taiga. According to a 2003 report, about 200 U.S. land bird species breed in the boreal forest and wetlands of

*Black spruce* (Picea mariana) *trees. They are common on the thin, nutrient-poor soils of the middle and northern Canadian taiga. Notice the lichen growing on the tree trunks and the fungi emerging from the soil around the trees in the foreground. Some trees in the middle distance have succumbed to natural damage or disease and have fallen.* (Courtesy of Jim Brandenburg/ Minden Pictures)

Canada every summer and migrate south to the United States in winter. They include warblers, finches, sparrows, and swifts, numbering several million birds in all. Among large plant-eating mammals of the taiga are caribou, moose, and wood bison, while brown and black bears are omnivorous (eat plants and animals). The large carnivores (meat-eaters) include the lynx, coyote, wolverine, and gray wolf.

The boreal forest is home to many Native Americans, with those of Algonquian descent traditionally living to the east, in areas extending around the Great Lakes and Hudson Bay regions, and eastward toward the coast. Those of Athabascan descent traditionally live in Alaska, along the Pacific coast, and in the Rocky Mountain region. Today, small communities dotted across the taiga subsist on extraction industries, such as forestry and mining, and to a lesser extent, on hunting, trapping, and tourism.

The major threats to Canada's forests are commercial logging for timber and wood pulp, oil and gas exploration, mining for precious minerals, and the building of dams to generate electricity (see sidebar below). More than three-quarters of Canada's logging is done by clear-cutting (removing all the trees in a given area). Unless planted with suitable saplings (young trees) such cleared areas are normally slow to recover and can be subject to severe soil erosion (see "Clear-cutting," pages 146–148). As timber supplies in the southern taiga become depleted, exploitation is moving northward to

## Threats to Canada's taiga

In 2000, Washington's World Resources Institute (WRI) reported that:

- Less than 3 percent of Canada's forest is closely protected from large-scale industrial activities.
- Only about one half of Canada's preindustrial taiga forest remains or is not threatened by removal.
- Almost 50 percent of Canada's taiga forest is under lease to forestry companies.

## Pacific coast rain forest

The coniferous forests that clothe the western mountain slopes along North America's Pacific coast, from Alaska to northern California, have a milder and wetter climate than the rest of the taiga. The coastal mountains block the chilly air traveling down from the Arctic, and, warmed by the sea, the coastal region has a mild climate, with temperatures rarely dropping below freezing (32°F; 0°C)—unusual for taiga. The coastal mountains also trap the moist wind blowing in from the Pacific and deflect the air upward, which causes the air to release much of its moisture as rain. The western slopes receive more than 10 feet (3 m) of rain each year. Not surprisingly, their forests are called rain forests. They contain similar species to those found elsewhere in North America's taiga—spruce, pine, fir, hemlock, and larch—but the forests are much more luxuriant. Their rich undergrowth of ferns, mosses, and lichens—growing on trees as well as on the ground—reminds visitors of tropical rain forests.

The rain forests of northern California and southwest Oregon are home to the world's largest trees. Here, giant conifers called coast redwoods (*Sequoia sempervirens*) infiltrate the normal mix of taiga trees. In northern California, one coast redwood has the distinction of being the world's tallest tree. At a recent count it was 367 feet (112 m) high, with a trunk 10 feet (3.17 m) across and bark about 12 inches (30 cm) thick. Felled trees of similar size have been dated from their growth rings at 2,200 years old.

wilderness areas. Currently, Canada is the world's largest exporter of wood-based products.

For decades, industries in Canada and the United States have been releasing fumes rich in the oxides of sulfur and nitrogen, which react with water vapor to produce acid rain. Environmental laws now curb the production of sulfur-rich fumes from the burning of oil and coal by industry, but many forested regions in southeast Canada are recovering only slowly. Acid rain attacks the needle leaves of conifers. It also changes the chemistry of soil water, making nutrients less available to trees and mobilizing metals that can prove toxic. The combined effects of acid rain weaken conifers, making them more liable to succumb to pests, diseases, or hard winters (see "Air pollution," pages 153–158).

## European taiga

European taiga stretches from Scotland in the west to the Ural Mountains of Russia in the east. Most of the European taiga—except for that in Scotland and in western parts of Norway—borders arctic tundra to the north. The most northerly taiga often consists of clumps of trees, especially larches, scattered among the tundra—the so-called *tree tundra* or *tundra forest*. The old, dense taiga of Fennoscandia (Norway, Sweden, and Finland) contains Scotch pine (*Pinus sylvestris*) and Norway spruce (*Picea abies*). Where forests have been cut down and natural regrowth occurs, birches and aspens tend to dominate. In western Russia, Siberian spruce (*Picea obovata*) dominates the old growth forest, with Siberian pine (*Pinus sibirica*) and Siberian larch (*Larix sibirica*) enriching the forest in the east.

*The distribution of taiga in Europe*

South of the dense taiga, the transitional zone, sometimes called southern taiga, consists of mixed conifer and broad-

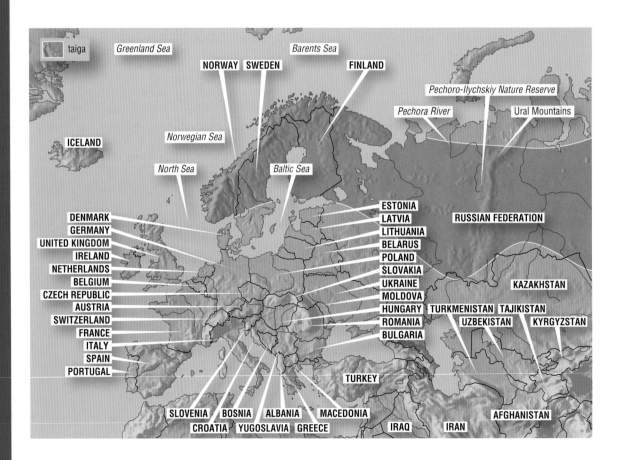

## Conifer forests in European mountains

Taiga-like conifer forests grow south of the taiga belt in the central European mountains of the Pyrenees and Alps. The forests contain the same species of pine and fir as are found farther north in the true taiga. In the high humidity of the northern Caucasus Mountains in Georgia, bordering Russia, grows the 260-feet (80-m)-high Caucasian fir (*Abies nordmanniana*). The rich, dark soils found here also support broad-leaved trees that grow as an understory beneath the lofty fir trees.

leaved forest. In many areas, taiga's southern boundary roughly coincides with the northern limit of distribution of the English oak tree (*Quercus robur*). Farther south, the taiga merges with broad-leaved forest in the west and central regions and gives way in the southeast to land cultivated as pasture, or for cereals or fodder. In high altitudes, however, taiga-like forests may grow instead (see the sidebar).

The taiga near the Atlantic coastline of Scandinavia is rather unusual. Here, the North Atlantic Drift, an ocean current fed by the Gulf Stream, keeps northwest Scandinavia unusually mild and wet. The growing season is about six months, although air temperatures rarely rise above 59°F (15°C). The taiga here reaches about 70°N—farther north than anywhere else in the world.

The mountains of Scandinavia cast a rain shadow to the east—an area of low rainfall on the downwind slope of a mountain. Moisture-laden air arriving from the west cools as it is deflected up western mountain slopes, unloading its moisture as precipitation. By the time this air descends the eastern flanks, its moisture load—and associated rainfall—is reduced.

The Baltic Shield in the east of European Russia is dominated by pine forests that grow on sandy and other crystalline deposits left as glaciers have retreated within the last 10,000 years. Spruce and fir trees, and to a lesser extent birch, cover the drier parts of the central plains. Compared with other parts of the world's taiga, the eastern European forests contain large numbers of small settlements, often close to rivers. At various times these settlements have been inhabited by hunters, loggers, small-scale farmers, and in some cases reindeer herders.

In Scotland, after several thousand years of forest clearance, the taiga has almost disappeared but for patches scattered across the highlands (see sidebar). Large taiga mammals such as the beaver, lynx, wolf, and brown bear became extinct through hunting and habitat loss at least several hundred years ago. Heather moors replaced the pine forests, and grazing by sheep and red deer prevented the regrowth of woodland. In the 20th century, the Forestry Commission created many plantations of non-British conifer species such as Sitka spruce and Norway spruce, which grew quickly and were easy to process into timber.

In much of western and central Fennoscandia, people have exploited the taiga only within the last 200 years. The emphasis here has been on logging for timber, with patches of forest clear-cut and trees of the same species and age being grown to replace them before they, too, are harvested. Such operations greatly reduce the biological diversity of the forest. In Sweden, for example, scientists have placed 1,900 forest species on the World Conservation Union (IUCN) Red List of endangered plants and animals. There are now moves to nurture a more diverse forest system for multiple use, including sport and recreational interests such as hunting, boating, and bird-watching, as well as timber production.

## Scotland's Caledonian Forest

An ancient conifer forest, the Caledonian Forest, covered about 20 percent of Scotland in prehistoric times. It originally contained only three species of conifer: the Scotch pine, the juniper, and the yew. Today, clearance by people has shrunk the forest to about 1 percent of its former size. The Forestry Commission now provides grants to encourage landowners to plant traditional species in the locality.

In European Russia, the taiga has been settled for thousands of years, but the lifestyles of the local peoples have not decimated the forest trees to the same extent as they have farther west. Nevertheless, human activities have strongly influenced the forest. People have set fires to clear the forest for agriculture—often to create hay meadows to feed cattle and other livestock. The forest has grown back in these areas but with an altered mix of tree species. Hunting and fishing have altered the community of animals. Hunting cabins lie dotted about the European Russian taiga and many are still used. Foresters have selectively logged high-value trees over much of the taiga within the last century.

## Siberian taiga

The Siberian taiga extends from the Ural Mountains in the west to the Verkhoyansk Mountains in the east, reaching a maximum width of about 1,000 miles (1,600 km) from north to south. It is the world's largest expanse of taiga.

The Ural Mountains block rain clouds from reaching the West Siberian Plain, so the climate here tends to be dry and typically continental, with hot summers and bitterly cold winters. Siberian spruce and Siberian pine thrive here, but broad-leaved trees have difficulty surviving the cold winters. They are barely present, except to the south in the transition zone between the taiga and the Russian steppe, where birch and aspen grow.

The climate of Siberia is strongly affected by anticyclones (high-pressure weather systems) that bring cold air masses from the Arctic (see "Air masses," pages 46–48). In western Siberia, the cold, wet weather encourages bogs to form over large areas. Farther south, in the Tien Shan Mountains of Kazakhstan, continental dryness combines with high altitudes to produce a short growing season, and only hardy trees survive (see the sidebar on page 17).

In central and eastern Siberia, between the Yenisey and Lena Rivers, the climate is typically continental, with summer temperatures higher than in western Siberia and less precipitation (rain, hail, and snow) throughout the year. With less snow to insulate the ground against the cold, the permafrost

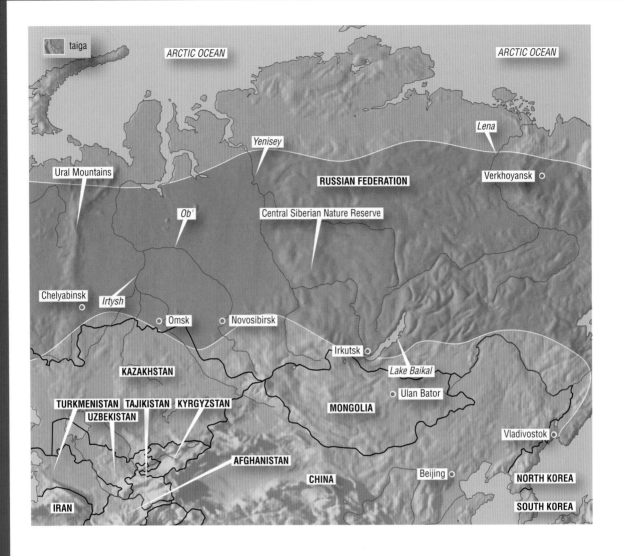

taiga

ARCTIC OCEAN

ARCTIC OCEAN

Lena

Yenisey

Verkhoyansk

Ural Mountains

RUSSIAN FEDERATION

Ob'

Central Siberian Nature Reserve

Chelyabinsk

Irtysh

Omsk

Novosibirsk

Irkutsk

Lake Baikal

KAZAKHSTAN

Ulan Bator

TURKMENISTAN   TAJIKISTAN   KYRGYZSTAN

UZBEKISTAN

MONGOLIA

Vladivostok

AFGHANISTAN

CHINA

Beijing

NORTH KOREA

IRAN

SOUTH KOREA

*The distribution of taiga in Siberia*

(permanently frozen ground) is thicker, starving the trees of available water in winter. The hardy Daurian larch thrives over much of north and central Siberia, but spruces, pines, and firs become common only in the south, where temperature changes are less extreme. Where logging or fire has removed the cover of conifer trees, birches are quick to invade.

East of the Lena River, but away from the moderating influence of the Pacific Ocean, the climate is more continental, with baking summers and freezing winters. The average temperature difference between January and July in Verkhoyansk is greater than 108°F (60°C). The lack of rainfall in summer

## The Tien Shan Mountains of central Asia

The Tien Shan Mountains in Kazakhstan harbor the Tien Shan spruce (*Pinus tienschanica*), which thrives despite lack of moisture in late summer. The tree halts its growth in early July, limiting its growing season to only 50–55 days. The spruce survives due to an exceptionally deep root system that not only seeks out any vestiges of water in the soil but also anchors the plant against strong winds.

favors grasses rather than forest in parts of eastern Siberia. Here lie expanses of grass-covered steppe (prairie), with stands of forest in between. In the mountains, the Siberian stone pine (*Pinus sibirica*) becomes the dominant tree. The lack of moisture and the mountainous landscape mean that there are far fewer bogs in eastern Siberia than in the west.

The Siberian taiga is probably the world's largest tract of old-growth forest; it is even larger in area than the Amazon rain forest. Central and eastern Siberia are home to Russia's greatest populations of large taiga mammals, including reindeer (caribou), elk (moose), wolves, red foxes, and brown bears. The Yenisey River acts as a boundary, preventing the movement of many larger animal species. Reindeer and moose are more common to the east than to the west, and at least 11 species of birds and mammals are found on the east side of the Yenisey but not on the west.

Logging, coal mining, and oil and gas exploration scar the southern Siberian taiga, and this development is inexorably moving slowly northward. Air pollution from metal-smelting plants has already damaged tracts of taiga forest, and the plants' metal-rich wastewater discharges have poisoned rivers. Several planned hydroelectric schemes threaten to drown parts of the southern taiga.

## Far Eastern taiga

The East Asian taiga stretches from the Verkhoyansk Mountains bordering eastern Siberia to the Sea of Okhotsk to the east and then, interrupted by tundra, to the isolated Kamchatka

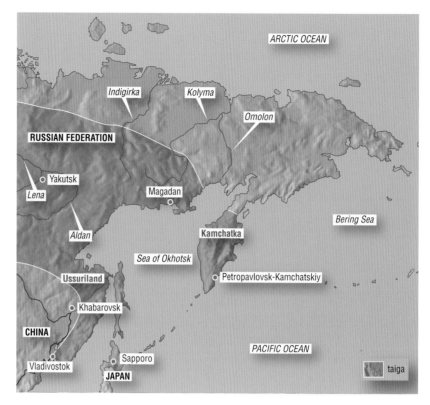

*The distribution of taiga in Far East Asia*

peninsula farther east. To the south, taiga extends to the mountainous regions of northeastern China and the Korean peninsula. On the northern Japanese island of Hokkaido, dense taiga forest continues as far south as 43°N.

The Kamchatka peninsula is a volcano-ridden wilderness interspersed by tumbling streams, swampy tundra, and patches of taiga. At 745 miles (1,200 km) long, and with an area almost the same as that of Japan, Kamchatka is inhabited by only about 300,000 people. The chilly Oyashio Current flowing from the north cools Kamchatka. Where this current meets the warm Kuroshio Current (or Japan Current) flowing from the south, the colliding currents generate sea mists. Kamchatka, as a result, has one of the gloomiest climates on Earth. Bouts of mist and drizzle punctuate the weather for nine months of the year, only clearing during the warmest months of summer.

The peculiar assortment of geological and climatic factors, coupled with a low human population, combine to perpetuate an unusual patchwork of taiga. Plants benefit from the volcanoes, which warm the soil and enrich it with nutrients. Larch and spruce grow in the lowlands. Stands of willow and stone birch, twisted into gnarled shapes by cold winds, grow along the coast. Kamchatka alder forms dense thickets on mountain slopes. The local silver fir species (*Abies gracilis*), a relict of preglacial times more than 100,000 years ago, is unique to Kamchatka. Today, it is restricted to a patch of forest covering less than 50 acres (20 ha). The rivers, which are free from dams and other human-made obstacles, become dense with fish when salmon arrive to spawn. At various times, five species of salmon (sockeye, pink, chum, silver, and king) ascend Kamchatka's rivers, providing a rich feast for Kamchatka's brown bears—the same species and the same giant size as Alaska's grizzly bears.

Siberia's eastern coastal regions and the land to the south called Ussuriland, extending from the Amur estuary in the north to the borders of China and Korea in the south, share a distinctive climate. The summer monsoon winds of East Asia bring mild weather and abundant rains from the Pacific Ocean, while the Siberian anticyclone dominates in winter, starving this region of rain and bringing icy temperatures. The summer abundance of moisture, coupled with cool winters, tends to displace the distribution of taiga southward, so that taiga grows at latitudes where, to the west in central Asia, deserts are found.

In northern parts of Ussuriland, spruce, birch, and creeping stone pine dominate the taiga, interspersed by stands of Korean pines (*Pinus koraiensis*), with their giant cones laden with up to 200 pine nuts (naked seeds), which are rich in oil. In winter, these nuts help sustain a diverse range of animals, including birds such as nutcrackers and woodpeckers and mammals ranging from squirrels and chipmunks to deer and wild boars. Top predators include brown bears (smaller than the Kamchatka variety), lynx, and wolverines.

Where the monsoon winds exert their greatest influence, yeddo spruce (*Picea jezoensis*) and Siberian white fir (*Abies nephrolepsis*) dominate. In the southern transitional zone around Russia's southeast border with China, the taiga

## East Asia's rare large mammals

Two of the world's most endangered large animals live in the Far East taiga: the Amur (Siberian) tiger (*Panthera tigris altaica*), the largest subspecies of tiger, and the Amur leopard (*Panthera pardus orientalis*). The Amur tiger has all but disappeared from China, Korea, and most of Siberia, and a small population estimated at less than 400 lives in the far east of Russia. This population is threatened by poaching. The tiger's skin, bones, and internal organs are used in traditional Asian medicine. A single carcass is worth many thousands of dollars on the international black market. In addition, the tiger's habitat and food supply are threatened by logging interests that plan to exploit the region's timber in violation of Russian laws and international conventions.

The largest remaining population of the Amur leopard—a subspecies of leopard that grows a thick, pale coat for the winter—lies between Vladivostok and the Chinese border. Although the leopard is protected, fires set by farmers to burn crop stubble sometimes set the forest alight, clearing the woodland, which takes many years to recover. Short of food and space, leopards sometimes attack the livestock in deer farms and then become the hunted quarry of farmers.

vegetation is unusually varied, with many species of trees, shrubs, and climbers growing in dark, acidic soils. These forests are home to some of the world's rarest land mammals (see sidebar).

# CHAPTER 2

# GEOLOGY OF THE TAIGA

Many forces—physical, chemical, and biological—sculpt the landscape. Some of these—violent weather, earthquakes, or volcanic eruptions—produce observable change in a matter of minutes. Weathering, the gradual wearing away of rock by physical, chemical and biological processes, produces noticeable change over time spans ranging from days to millions of years. Some of the most far-reaching changes, those that create the major contours of the land in the first place, from rising mountains to deep gorges, operate over millions of years. They concern the structure and processes of the Earth deep beneath our feet.

## Earth's structure

Although most of the ground we walk upon feels solid, it is, in reality, a skin of rock only a few miles thick. This skin, called the *crust,* together with a slightly deeper layer of solid rock, called the *outer mantle,* is gradually moving over a plastic (slowly deforming) layer deeper in the Earth, called the *asthenosphere.* The crust and rigid outer mantle—together called the *lithosphere*—gradually creep across the surface of the planet at rates of one to six inches (2.5–15 cm) a year. Over millions of years, they carry the continents (major landmasses) with them, so the shape and arrangement of landmasses and oceans change.

The continents, and the oceans between them, lie upon wide chunks of crust called plates or tectonic plates (from the Greek *tecton,* meaning "to build"). There are about 20 plates in all, and about a dozen of these are very large—hundreds or thousands of miles across. The plates fit together like a giant jigsaw puzzle covering the surface of the Earth. At the boundaries between one plate and another, the plates crash

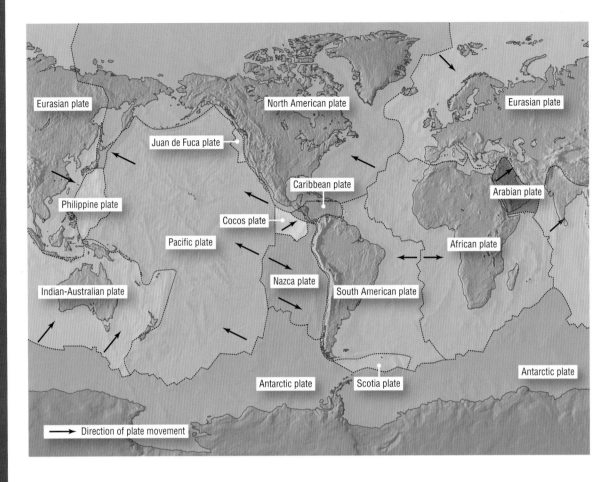

*Earth's plates. These are gigantic, slowly moving slabs of Earth's lithosphere.*

together, grind past one another, or move apart, but in slow motion. Most plates move sideways about one to two inches (2.5–5 cm) a year—slightly faster than the rate at which human fingernails grow.

Where two plates collide, the heavier one sinks beneath the lighter one. This happens, for example, where the heavier part of a plate under the ocean meets a lighter plate making up part of a continent. The oceanic crust sinks beneath the continental crust. As this happens, the continental crust buckles, like the folding edge of a sliding rug. This deformation uplifts mountains. The mountain ranges that run parallel to the Pacific coast of North America were created this way. These ranges, which include the Coast, Cascade, and Rocky Mountains, are still rising as the Pacific plate slides beneath the North American plate. At the same time, as oceanic crust sinks deep into the ground, high temperatures deep within the Earth warm it. The crust melts, creating molten rock, called *magma,* which may find its way back to the surface through a volcano. The Mount St. Helens volcano, which erupted in 1980, killing about 60 people and flattening nearly 500 square miles (1,300 km$^2$) of prime timber forest, is fed by magma that originated from the sinking crust off the Pacific coast.

Where plates slide past each other, their edges tend to snag rather than slide smoothly. Pressure builds underground at the boundary where the plates try to slide but friction keeps them locked together. Eventually, the pressure builds so high that the plates suddenly slip, and the pressure is released, sending shock waves through the ground. We feel these waves as earth tremors or earthquakes. The San Andreas Fault, which runs near San Francisco, is the sliding boundary between the North American and Pacific plates. In fact, both plates are moving northward, but the Pacific plate progresses at a faster pace than the North American. Every year, there are many minor earth tremors as the plates shift suddenly against each other. Every few decades, the earth tremors are bigger than normal, producing earthquakes that damage property and take lives. In 1906, a major earthquake in San Francisco toppled more than half of the city's buildings. Another major earthquake in 1989 shook the ground from southern Oregon to Los Angeles, toppling freeways.

Where two plates move apart, their motion creates space for new material to rise from deep in the Earth to fill gaps. Most of these plate boundaries lie beneath the ocean, and as they move apart, magma from deep within the crust or mantle rises to lay down new seafloor. Off the Pacific coast of North America, this is happening in the Juan de Fuca ridge. Here the Pacific plate is gradually creeping away from the Juan de Fuca plate, which itself is descending beneath the North American plate.

What causes the plates to move? Geologists, scientists who study the structure of the Earth and its processes of change, suspect that deep in the Earth, the asthenosphere contains heat-stirred currents called *convection currents.* These are mass movements of material generated by temperature differences.

Heat is generated by the radioactive breakdown of substances deep in the Earth that warm the plastic material in the asthenosphere. This plastic rock becomes less dense and so slowly rises toward Earth's surface. Blocked by the lithosphere, the material is forced to move horizontally. When it cools sufficiently and its density increases once again, it descends to approximately the level at which it began, so producing a circuit. The plates are riding on the back of the horizontal movement of these slow currents.

## North American landforms today

If a person were to walk across Canada, from Vancouver Island on the Pacific coast to Newfoundland on the Atlantic coast, he or she would cover about 3,000 miles (4,800 km) and have a roller-coaster journey rising up mountains and plunging into valleys along the way. The first obstacles would be the Coast Mountains and, behind them, the Rocky Mountains rising to 13,000 feet (4,000 m), both uplifted within the last 80 million years by the Pacific plate colliding with, and sliding under, the North American and other plates. Beyond the mountains, to the east, the traveler would come to the fertile Great Plains and Central Lowlands that form Canada's prairies. Much of Canada's wheat- and grain-fed cattle are farmed here. The prairies are covered with deposits up to one mile (1.6 km) deep left behind by retreating glaciers. To the northeast of these fertile plains lies the Canadian Shield, the heart of the continent, containing ancient rocks more than 2 billion years old.

About 600 million years ago, the Canadian Shield was a region of active mountain building, but since then the mountains have been worn away by scraping glaciers and by the combined effects of weathering. Today the Canadian Shield is a giant plain pockmarked by lakes and gentle hummocks (rounded, small hills). To the north lies Hudson Bay, a giant depression in the rock formed beneath the weight of an ice sheet and now filled with seawater from the Atlantic Ocean. To the east the ancient Laurentian Mountains lie between the Canadian Shield and the coastal plain. These mountains were covered with sediment before erosion exposed them. The present-day landforms of this part of Canada demonstrate clearly the combined effects of tectonic processes and of weathering and erosion over time. To the west, with a plate boundary nearby, the mountains are younger and taller. To the east, far distant from the nearest plate boundary, the mountains are old and low. With mountainous barriers to the west, the rivers of the Canadian lowlands drain eastward to the Atlantic Ocean or northward to the Arctic Ocean.

Northern Europe and northern Asia show similar features, with mountains uplifted where plates once came together or continue to do so, and shields of ancient rock that have been worn down into plains over millions of years. Like North America, they, too, have been scoured repeatedly by glaciers. The Urals, which separate European Russia from Siberia (part of Asia), were raised more than 280 million years ago when the East European and Siberia plates came together and folded the crust. The Baltic Shield of Scandinavia and north-western Russia includes Europe's oldest rock.

## The work of glaciers

Glaciers are often referred to as "rivers of ice." The glaciers that slide down mountain valleys are certainly like this. They form in highlands where winter snowfall does not melt away in summer. The snow gradually builds, squeezing the snow beneath to ice, and the ice and snow then flow downhill under the flow of gravity. These are valley glaciers.

But glaciers can be much bigger, engulfing almost an entire continent. Today, ice and snow cover about 80 percent of Greenland and 90 percent of Antarctica. These giant glaciers are not confined to valleys but smother almost an entire landmass in a thick sheet of ice. No wonder they are called continental glaciers, or *ice sheets*. The Greenland ice sheet is about 10,500 feet (3,200 m) thick at its center; the Antarctic sheet, about 9,850 feet (3,000 m) thick. Only 20,000 years ago, ice sheets like these covered more than half of North America and much of northern Eurasia. Twenty thousand years ago, the landscape where taiga grows today lay under a sheet of ice hundreds or thousands of feet thick.

Glaciers need cold and snow to build. Today, such conditions exist at high latitudes (polar and subpolar regions). These regions are cold because the Sun is lower in the sky here and strikes Earth's surface at a shallow angle (see "Solar heating and air movement," pages 39–40).

Glaciers also form at high altitudes in latitudes nearer the equator. The layer of the atmosphere nearest the Earth is cooler at high altitude than at low. Close to the equator, glaciers can form above altitudes of 18,000 feet (about 5,500 m). Near the poles, given the availability of snow, glaciers form near sea level.

The compacted ice in a glacier behaves almost like rock. In fact, to a geologist, glacial ice *is* rock made up of ice crystals. Buried in a glacier, with more snow piling on top, snowflakes—single, fluffy crystals of ice—become compacted together into a solid mass of giant crystals.

The snow in a glacier flows in slow motion—like thick honey spreading over a slice of bread, but even slower. Where a glacier is thicker and the slope steeper, the glacier will flow more quickly. Glacial ice flows in two ways. In particularly cold regions, most movement is by sheets of ice crystals slipping against one another. The ice is frozen to the ground, and as the ice crystals shift, they pull up any loose rock or soil to which they are anchored. This kind of movement is called *plastic flow.*

In slightly warmer environments, warmth in the ground and the pressure of ice pressing down from above (increasing pressure lowers melting point) may be enough to melt a thin bottom layer of glacial ice. The overlying snow and ice can slide on this liquid layer. This kind of movement, called *basal slip,* occurs in the fastest-moving parts of valley glaciers. The pioneering Swiss geologist and zoologist Louis Agassiz (1807–73) measured a valley glacier to flow as fast as 245 feet (about 75 m) in a year. Agassiz went on to become a founding member of the U.S. National Academy of Sciences and a regent of the Smithsonian Institution. Modern satellite measurements of the Antarctic continental glacier as it leaves the South Pole give speeds of flow of about 26 feet (8 m) a year. However, some ice flows break off the main Antarctic ice sheet and form "ice streams" that flow at a 100 times this rate. Even so, this movement—very fast by the standards of most glaciers—would not be visible to the eye.

Glaciers may flow slowly, but they are immensely powerful. The power of a glacier is concealed beneath its smooth surface. As it flows, its bottom and sides tear at the rock. An average-size glacier 1,000 or so feet across is equivalent to a fleet of dozens of bulldozers. When glacial ice meets cracked rock, it engulfs the rock and breaks it free. The boulder then becomes a weapon that grinds against bedrock as it is carried along by the glacier. The glacier, with its load of plucked rocks, grinds the rocks against the valley sides. In time, rocks the size of houses become ground down to boulders the size of small cars. Smaller boulders and fragments broken off the larger boulders become ground down to silt and clay called, appropriately, "rock flour." When the melting ice at the edge of a glacier leaves behind this dust, it dries and can be blown away on the wind to settle as *loess* (windblown silt).

As glaciers move across the landscape, and then retreat when the climate warms, the grinding action of the glaciers' load of rocks leaves telltale scratch marks, called *striations,* in the underlying rock. The striations follow the direction of ice movement. Geologists can work out the flow patterns of long-gone continental glaciers by studying the pattern of striations on present-day rocks.

Other features in the landscape give clues to the direction and extent of flow of ancient glaciers. Glaciers leave behind small hills (hillocks) of bedrock called *roches moutonées* (French for "sheep rocks" because their shape resembles the contours of a sheep's back). These have a smooth, gentle slope on the upcurrent side, where the glacier's ice has flowed past, and a steep, ragged edge on the downcurrent side, where the glacier has pulled out fragments of rock.

Piles of assorted rubble and small particles left behind by glaciers are called *moraines*. The pile left by the leading edge of a glacier when it melts back and recedes is called an end or terminal moraine. It forms a distinctive curved deposit where the glacier once reached.

Ice melting within glaciers produces streams flowing within and beneath the ice. They transport, sort, and deposit some of the glacial debris. Such deposits, called *outwash,* tend to contain particles of more uniform size than are found on moraines, because of the sorting action of the moving water.

The features left behind by glacial action create a variety of environmental conditions that favor different types of taiga vegetation. Where depressions are left behind, lakes and bogs form, which commonly proceed in a succession from sphagnum moss bogs, through reeds and shrubs, to broad-leaved trees, and then conifers such as black spruce. Where outwash has left sand behind, it produces well-drained soils where pines are likely to flourish at the expense of other conifers.

Within the last 70,000 years, glaciers have moved south across North America and northern Eurasia, scraping off the soil. Most of the soils within taiga regions have developed within the last 10,000 years in the transported materials left behind by the receding glaciers.

## Taiga soils

Most taiga soils are *podzols.* The name comes from the Russian words *pod,* meaning "under," and *zola,* meaning "ash." Ash-like is a good description of the soil's texture and gray color just beneath the surface. In the U.S. system of soil classification, podzol is referred to as *spodosol.*

Podzols develop in the cool, wet conditions of the taiga. Cool temperatures slow the activities of microbes that break down the pine needles and other plant and animal remains that settle on the forest floor. As a result, just beneath the ground surface is a layer rich in *humus*—partly decayed animal and plant matter. At the same time, precipitation is much greater than evaporation. In other words, over the course of a year, the water falling to the ground is greater in volume than the water that evaporates into the air from the ground surface. Such conditions cause an overall downward movement of water through the soil. As the water drains downward it takes dissolved plant nutrients, such as nitrates and phosphates, with it. The breakdown products of plants trap metals and carry them deeper into the ground. This overall process of soluble substances being carried away from the upper soil by downward-percolating water is called *leaching,* and its effect is that the near-surface soil becomes poor in

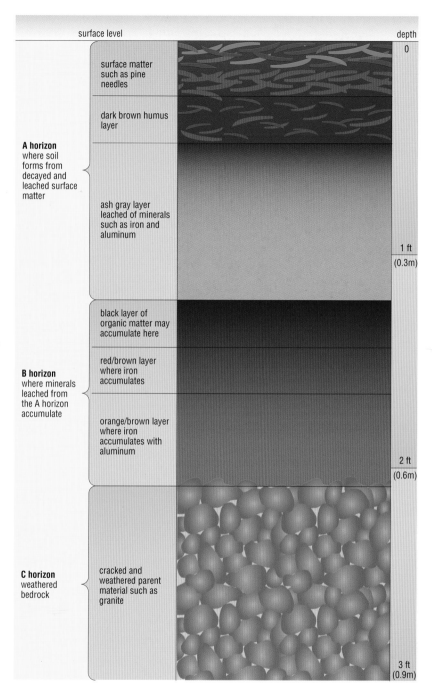

surface level

depth

surface matter
such as pine
needles

dark brown humus
layer

**A horizon**
where soil
forms from
decayed and
leached surface
matter

ash gray layer
leached of minerals
such as iron and
aluminum

0

1 ft
(0.3m)

black layer of
organic matter may
accumulate here

**B horizon**
where minerals
leached from
the A horizon
accumulate

red/brown layer
where iron
accumulates

orange/brown layer
where iron
accumulates with
aluminum

2 ft
(0.6m)

**C horizon**
weathered
bedrock

cracked and
weathered parent
material such as
granite

3 ft
(0.9m)

*Podzol, the most typical
soil of a conifer forest*

nutrients. The soil is also highly acidic, with pHs typically in
the 3.5–4.5 range (see the sidebar "Acidity and acid rain,"
page 156). The main reason for this is that the rock over

which taiga forms is typically rich in silica, the main constituent of sand. As the rock breaks down by weathering, silica-rich particles tend to produce acid soils. The remains of conifer trees, which fungi decompose to release acids, tend to maintain or even raise the acidity of the soil. These nutrient-poor, highly acid conditions favor the growth of conifers over most broad-leaved plants.

A typical podzol has a dark brown humus-rich top layer with a clay-rich gray layer extending for a foot or so beneath, from which much of the metals and plant nutrients have been washed out. Beneath the gray layer is often a thin layer of nutrient-rich material leached out of the humus, and below that a reddish brown layer rich in iron and aluminum deposited by the descending acidic water. The metal-rich layer may eventually become so compacted that little water can penetrate it. If so, the soil above the layer may become waterlogged, providing ideal conditions for the creation of peat (a dark brown layer of partially decayed plant remains). The reddish brown metal-rich layer typically rests upon weathered glacial deposits or bedrock.

The podzol's top layers, which are rich in decaying leaf litter, and the deeper layer, which is rich in nutrients, are the main sources of nutrients for taiga plants, and roots gravitate to these regions. Many conifers produce small seeds—among them are larches, fir, and pines—and these do not germinate well among the leaf litter on the forest floor. The young plants grow best on the decaying wood of tree trunks or branches that have fallen in the forest.

## Bogs, peat, and forest

Bogs are low-lying areas where the ground is soaked in water for part or all of the year. The spongy mixture of vegetation, water, and soil can be treacherous underfoot for any people or animals that wander into them.

In bogs, the presence of excess water in the soil slows down the entry of oxygen from the air. This, in turn, moderates the activities of microbes that break down vegetation. Coupled with the cold conditions of the taiga, this slow decomposition encourages the formation of peat—a dark brown layer of plant remains that are partly decomposed. Given millions of years, accumulations of peat may become buried underground and compressed to form coal deposits. Some taiga peoples use dried peat itself as a low-grade fuel source. Not just vegetation, but animal remains and human artifacts decompose sluggishly in peat. The preserved remains—plant, animal, and human—thus offer a time capsule of the climate and history of a region (see the sidebar "Hidden history").

When peat deposits form, they harbor large quantities of nutrients that are not readily recycled. In many cases, the plants that grow on peat bogs have to cope with lack of nutrients as well as lack of oxygen. The variety of plant life is fairly small, and those that survive are specialists, such as sphagnum mosses (see "Sphagnum moss," page 71) and insect-consuming pitcher plants (see the sidebar "Deadly pitchers").

Taiga bogs often form where glaciers leave depressions in the ground that fill with water to form lakes. Sphagnum mosses, which can survive the meager supply of nutrients and the oxygen-poor conditions, colonize the edges of the lake. As the sphagnum mosses advance to the center of the lake, the area of open water shrinks. Sphagnum grows upward to the light, depriving lower layers of moss the available sunlight.

## Hidden history

Scientists can unlock taiga's recent history from the pollen grains preserved in its peat. Pollen grains—the microscopic capsules released from the flowers of trees and other plants—are armor-plated. A tough coat protects the male sex cell inside and, fortuitously, also enables pollen grains to be preserved more or less intact for thousands of years.

When scientists excavate peat, they take samples from different layers and examine them under a microscope to identify and count the pollen grains they contain. The variety and abundance of pollen tell scientists which trees once grew nearby and the overall balance of plants in the local community. The deeper the peat layer, the older it is. By comparing the pollen content of different layers, scientists can follow how a local plant community has changed over thousands of years. Because climate influences vegetation, pollen profiles also give them insight into how local climate has changed over the millennia.

## Deadly pitchers

Insect-eating plants often thrive in peat bogs. In these waterlogged conditions, where oxygen is lacking and nutrients are in poor supply, carnivorous plants can obtain extra nutrients by trapping and digesting animals. The pitcher plant (genus *Nepenthes*), for example, has green leaves that trap sunlight to make food. But some of its leaves are sculpted into jug-shaped vessels, hence the plant's name. The plant secretes nectar at the top of its water-filled pitchers. Attracted insects slide down the slippery necks of the pitchers and drown. Bacteria decompose the insect carcasses, and the plant absorbs the released nutrients. Some plant species even secrete acids into the pitcher liquid to speed the digestive process.

The light-starved moss beneath dies and adds to the peat. Gradually, the accumulating peat turns the edges of the lake into a spongy bog, which rises higher and begins to dry out as the peat layer grows. Rushes colonize the margins of the lake. In time, shrubs and trees take root in what was once boggy ground. Eventually, large conifers penetrate to the center of the former lake. Forest has replaced open water.

### Permafrost

Across much of the northern and eastern taiga in both North America and Eurasia, the ground a few feet beneath the surface remains permanently frozen. Called *permafrost,* this frozen layer reaches considerably more than 1,000 feet (300 m) thick in parts of Alaska, northern Canada, and much of eastern Siberia. Below the permafrost, warmth from deeper parts of the Earth ensures the ground remains unfrozen.

Permafrost strongly influences the vegetation in more than one-third of the taiga region. It blocks the downward flow of water through the ground, encourages rainfall to run off the land, and tends to make soils waterlogged. When the top layer of permafrost thaws in summer and then refreezes in winter from the top down, it causes great stresses in the ground that lead to *frost heave.* The soil expands and rises in a small hummock up to 20 inches (50 cm) high. This disruption

sphagnum moss colonizing the edge of the lake and creating boggy ground

lake formed from water filling a depression

peat forming at the bottom of the lake

sphagnum mosses growing toward the center of the lake

reeds colonizing the edges of the boggy ground

peat filling a large proportion of the depression

only small areas of open water remain

conifer trees growing on the former bog

*Three stages in the ecological succession from a lake and bog to a conifer forest* can be enough to uproot trees. Frost heave is caused by lens-shaped blocks of ice forming near the soil surface as freezing air temperatures penetrate the soil. Water expands when it freezes, and in heavily wetted soil, more water is drawn toward the accumulating ice, which freezes, so the ice block grows. This creates an ice-filled space in the soil, which pushes the overlying soil upward. When the thaw comes, the ice block gradually melts, but the space vacated by it may be filled with soil shifting in from the sides as well as from above, so the effect of frost heaving is to partially mix the soil. In patches, this mixing pushes deeper layers of soil toward the surface. Repeated year after year, frost heave can substantially mix the soil to depths of well over 12 inches (30 cm).

In soils affected by permafrost, the water may rise or sink through the soil depending on the season of the year and the balance between thawing and freezing in the surface layers. This can cause podzol to become less obviously compartmentalized into its constituent layers as deposited substances rise and fall with the prevailing direction of water travel.

Permafrost causes problems in projects that involve excavating the ground, such as oil prospecting or building construction. Digging exposes permafrost to warm air, and the top layer of permafrost melts. Because the water cannot drain through the frozen ground beneath, it stays in the soil. The waterlogged soil then behaves like a slow-moving liquid and sags or creeps, causing problems for those constructing roads, buildings, factories, or pipelines. For decades in cold parts of Siberia, people have been building their houses on raised supports so that the warmth from their dwellings does not thaw the permafrost. Engineers designing the Alaska pipeline, which brings oil south to the United States, likewise decided to build long stretches raised above ground and insulated from it to avoid the problem of the permafrost melting. When Siberian prospectors developed similar aboveground pipelines but failed to insulate them properly from the ground, the pipelines buckled and split, causing oil-pollution incidents. They had not learned the lessons of their compatriots.

The current taiga biome has developed on a landscape previously gouged by advancing glaciers and overlaid with deposits left by retreating ice. This geological process has been repeated many times within the last 2 million–3 million years (the Pleistocene epoch, ending some 11,000 years ago). The last reshaping took place within the last 70,000 years. During that time, the most recent glaciation (a period when glaciers and ice sheets were extensive in North America and northern Eurasia) peaked about 20,000 years before the present. The current interglacial (a warmer period between glaciations) began about 11,000 years ago. Called the Flandrian, it corresponds with the Holocene or Recent epoch. Within the last 11,000 years, as the ice has retreated, the depressions left behind have filled with rainwater to form numerous lakes. Sands and lighter grains left behind by glaciers have blown on the wind, being swept away in some places and gathering in others. Taiga soils are young and shallow, having developed on bedrock or deposits within the last 10,000 years. Variation in the underlying material and its drainage produces some irregularity in soil conditions. Some sites are dry, others wet, some nutrient-rich, others nutrient-poor. This variability has helped establish the diversity of plant communities found in the taiga today.

# CHAPTER 3

# TAIGA CLIMATE

Taiga develops where temperatures are cold for much of the year but the climate is humid (the air is moist). Over the course of a year, water falling to the ground from precipitation (dew, rain, snow, sleet, or hail) is greater than that lost to the air by evaporation (liquid water turning to vapor) and sublimation (frozen water turning directly to vapor). As a result, the ground tends to be damp. Where drainage is poor, wetlands form.

Most taiga trees are extraordinarily resistant to cold but can also tolerate heat, providing it is accompanied by humidity. Temperatures in eastern Siberia can drop to –76°F (–60°C) in winter and peak at –104°F (–40°C)—an astonishing temperature range of 180°F (100°C) over the year. Such extremes do not stop the Daurian larch from eking out a living.

A key requirement for taiga trees is moist air in the summer months. Without it, they lose water too rapidly through their needlelike leaves and cannot grow to a large size even if the ground is moist. In the dry air in Tbilisi Botanical Garden, Georgia (part of the former USSR), spruces grow to a height of only 33 feet (10 m). In their normal taiga environment, such trees would reach more than 100 feet (30 m).

## Weather, climate, and atmosphere

*Weather* is the blend of sun and rain, wind and calm, cloudy and clear skies, and other features of the air around us that we experience from day to day and week to week. Weather includes technical features that scientists measure, such as air pressure (the pressure of the column of air pressing down on Earth's surface), humidity (a measure of how much moisture the air contains), and evaporation (how quickly water is being turned to water vapor at Earth's surface).

*Climate* refers to the average of weather patterns from year to year and decade to decade. It is the longer-term pattern of temperature, air pressure, precipitation, cloudiness, wind speeds, and so on, in a particular region. People talk of the climate of the Great Lakes region of Canada and the United States. On the other hand, they call the overall trends in weather patterns across the world the *global climate*.

The *atmosphere* is the blanket of air wrapped around Earth's surface. It is about 560 miles (900 km) high at the equator and slightly lower at the poles. It is Earth's lifeline and protector. The atmosphere contains the oxygen people breathe and that most plants, animals, and microscopic organisms need for respiration (the process of breaking down food substances to release energy). Its clouds feed the land with water circulated from the sea. It acts as an insulating blanket, ensuring that the Earth neither warms nor cools too rapidly for the survival of life. Weather and climate are features of the circulating air in the lower part of Earth's atmosphere, called the *troposphere*.

*At the northern edges of the taiga belt the conditions are harsh and the trees are stunted and grow thinly, as shown here, in Alaska. In the foreground, a caribou (Rangifer tarandus) mother and her calf are crossing a snowy field. (Courtesy of Michael Quinton/Minden Pictures)*

# What is radiation?

Many people think of radiation as the harmful rays or particles associated with nuclear weapons and nuclear power plants. However, these kinds of radiation—called *ionizing radiation*—are only part of a wide range of types, many of which, far from being harmful, are beneficial to humans and other life-forms.

Most forms of radiation are *electromagnetic*—they have both electrical and magnetic properties—and travel through the atmosphere or space as electromagnetic waves. The range, or *spectrum,* of electromagnetic radiation extends from radio waves with long wavelengths to ultraviolet (UV) waves with short wavelengths. Between these two extremes lies a range of wavelengths that are visible to the human eye—the visible spectrum of light—that includes all the colors of the rainbow. Sunlight includes all wavelengths of visible light, plus some people cannot see directly, such as UV light and infrared light. UV light can be harmful because it is readily absorbed by nucleic acids, the major constituent of genes—the cell components that determine inherited characteristics. The absorbed energy can alter nucleic acids, causing mutations that can lead to cancer and other disruptions to normal life processes.

Ionizing radiation includes those radioactive particles or rays (alpha and beta particles, and gamma rays) released by the decay of radioactive substances such as radium, uranium, and plutonium. Cosmic rays (high-energy particles reaching the Earth from space) and X-rays (high-energy waves produced by astronomical bodies, such as stars, and by artificial means) are also types of ionizing radiation. *Ionizing* refers to their ability to transfer energy to a neutral atom or molecule, so changing it into a negatively or positively charged ion. Such changes, taking place in the complex chemicals that make up living organisms, mean that ionizing radiations are usually harmful in anything other than small doses.

The atmosphere is also a protective barrier. A middle layer of the atmosphere, called the *stratosphere,* contains oxygen that absorbs ultraviolet (UV) radiation in sunlight (see sidebar). As it absorbs this radiation, the oxygen ($O_2$) is converted to ozone ($O_3$). The presence of the ozone layer in the stratosphere is a sign that harmful UV radiation has been absorbed. High levels of UV radiation can trigger mutations (spontaneous changes in the genetic material of cells) that can lead to cancer.

# Solar heating and air movement

The unequal heating of Earth's surface by the Sun (solar heating) drives global patterns of weather and climate. Lying between the tropic of Cancer in the Northern Hemisphere (23.5°N) and the tropic of Capricorn in the Southern Hemisphere (23.5°S) is that region of the Earth where the Sun is directly overhead in the sky for at least one day a year. The region is called the Tropics. It is markedly warmer than the poles because it receives more sunlight, both in terms of intensity and duration. Three main factors explain this difference.

First, near the equator, the midday Sun rises high in the sky, and the Sun's rays are angled almost directly downward. By contrast, near the poles, the midday Sun rises low in the sky and the Sun's rays hit Earth's surface at a shallow angle. At the poles, sunlight is more likely to bounce off the atmosphere or off Earth's surface rather than be absorbed.

Second, the sunlight that is absorbed at the poles is spread over a wider area of Earth's curved surface. A person can test this using a globe. Standing next to the globe and shining a flashlight beam onto the globe's surface from one side (as though the Sun were directly above the equator) produces a tight circle of light at the equator. Keeping the flashlight horizontal but moving it upward slightly so that it shines toward the North Pole produces a broad oval of light spread over a wider area of Earth's curved surface. As demonstrated with the flashlight, the brightness of light striking the poles is less than that reaching the Tropics. The same principle applies to sunlight.

The third factor is the amount of sunlight absorbed or reflected depending on Earth's *albedo* (its paleness or darkness). At the poles, ice and snow are present. These materials reflect sunlight well, so less heat is absorbed. In the Tropics, the landmasses are green, brown, or yellow, and the sea is mostly blue. These colors reflect less light and absorb more of the Sun's heat energy.

If the Tropics heat up more than the poles, why don't tropical regions simply get hotter and hotter? They do not because the moving oceans and atmosphere carry heat to other parts of the globe.

The air hugging Earth's surface warms by *conduction*—the transfer of heat energy into the air by direct contact with the ground. When air warms, it becomes less dense and rises. When it cools, it becomes denser and sinks. The unequal heating of Earth's surface by the Sun, with air rising in some places and sinking in others, causes the atmosphere to circulate over the planet's surface.

As tropical air warms, it rises. Low-level cool air moves in from higher latitudes (away from the Tropics) and replaces the air that has risen. Meanwhile, the warm air rises until it hits the *tropopause* (the cool boundary layer between troposphere and stratosphere). The air then travels across the upper troposphere toward the poles. As air rises through the atmosphere the weight of the column of air above it lessens. As the air pressure lessens, the rising air expands. The constituent molecules within the air move farther apart and collide less frequently. Collisions release heat energy, so fewer of them produce a cooling effect that chills the air—a phenomenon called *adiabatic cooling* (from the Greek *adiabatos,* meaning "impassable," referring to the heat loss or gain being self-generated). The air of the upper troposphere also cools as it moves sideways because it radiates heat through the upper atmosphere and into space. As the air chills, it becomes denser and gradually sinks, providing cool air that descends at higher latitudes but will later return toward the Tropics. Put simply, there is an overall movement of warm air from the Tropics toward the poles at high altitude. There is a return flow of cooler air at low altitude, from the poles toward the equator.

The English physicist Edmund Halley (1656–1742) was the first to suggest this simple model of global air movement in 1686. Another Englishman, George Hadley (1686–1768), modified the model in the 1750s, when he recognized that the Earth's rotation would alter the direction of airflow.

## The effect of Earth's rotation

The Earth spins on its axis. If a person could hover above the North Pole, he or she would see the Earth below spinning counterclockwise, rotating once every 24 hours. Earth's rotation causes most large-scale movements of water and wind on Earth's surface to turn rather than traveling in straight lines. This effect was investigated and described by the French mathematician Gustave-Gaspard de Coriolis (1792–1843) in the 1830s, and it now bears his name.

To understand the Coriolis effect, it helps to use a model globe (or at least to imagine a globe in the mind's eye). The Earth spins counterclockwise as seen from above the North Pole. For one rotation of the Earth, a point on the equator travels a lot farther through space (it follows a wider circle) than a point near the North Pole. The speed of rotation of a point at the equator is about 1,037 mph (1,670 km/h). A point in New York City, near latitude 40°N, rotates at about

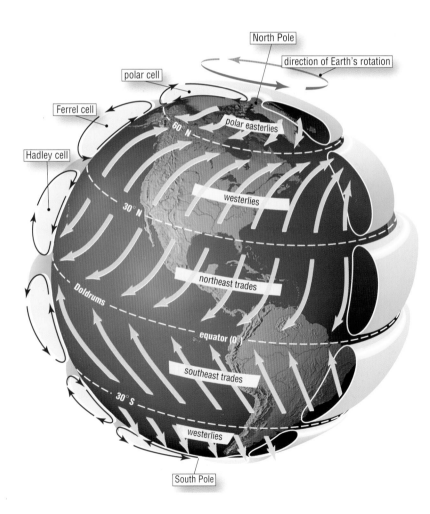

*Global air circulation. Rising or falling air masses at different latitudes produce major wind systems at Earth's surface, which are turned by the Coriolis effect.*

794 mph (1,280 km/h). This means that as an object attempts to fly or sail directly northward from the equator, it experiences a slower speed of rotation. This has the effect of deflecting its movement to the right. An easy way to see (or imagine this) is with a finger slowly moving toward the pole as it rests gently on the globe turning counterclockwise. The finger marks out a curved line moving toward the right.

Moving air experiences this turning effect, with the result that northward-moving winds are deflected to the right (or eastward) in the Northern Hemisphere. Winds moving northward form westerlies (winds that blow from the west). Southward-moving winds, because they are meeting higher speeds of rotation, are deflected to the left (or westward) in this hemisphere. They form easterlies or northeasterlies (winds that blow from the east or northeast respectively). In the Southern Hemisphere, Earth's rotation generates reliable westerly or easterly winds at similar latitudes to those in the Northern Hemisphere.

## Global air circulation

Hadley's model and the Coriolis effect offer a reasonable explanation for observed winds and climatic patterns in some parts of the world, particularly above open stretches of the ocean. Here, landmasses are absent that would deflect wind patterns and would heat and cool at different rates to water, so complicating patterns of air circulation.

Applying Hadley's model, around the equator—between latitudes 5°S and 10°N—warm, humid air rises because of the intense solar heating effect. This creates a belt of low pressure along the equator called the *intertropical convergence zone* (ITCZ). The rising air at the equator creates an upper-level high-pressure zone that deflects the tropical wind systems that arrive from either side of the equator. At the ITCZ, tropical wind systems from the two hemispheres come together, or converge, hence its name.

When rising tropical air reaches the tropopause (the boundary layer between troposphere and stratosphere), it turns poleward. By about 30°N or 30°S, the air has cooled sufficiently—by the radiation of heat into space—to sink back down to Earth's surface. These regions of subsiding air, called *subtropical anticyclones,* are high-pressure systems with characteristically warm, dry, still conditions. The warmth is created by the reverse process of adiabatic cooling: *adiabatic warming.* As cool air descends through the lower atmosphere, the weight of air above it increases; air pressure rises. The constituent molecules of the air are squeezed closer together, they collide more often, releasing heat energy, and so the air warms. On land, the world's great hot deserts—such as Africa's Sahara and Kalahari—are found in the subtropics, around latitudes 30°N and 30°S.

Air moving at low altitude from the subtropical anticyclones toward the equator is deflected by the Coriolis effect. These moving air masses create the famous trade winds that are among the steadiest, most reliable winds. Near the equator, the trade winds die out as they meet the rising air associated with the ITCZ. British sailors used to call this region the Doldrums (from an old English word meaning "dull"). Seafarers feared becoming becalmed (kept motionless by lack of wind) here. The air circulations that rise at the ITCZ and descend at the subtropical anticyclones are called *Hadley cells,* named after George Hadley.

The descending air at around 30°latitude diverges, with part moving poleward rather than toward the equator. This poleward-moving air feeds a circulation of air between latitudes 30° and 60°, called *Ferrel cells,* after the American meteorologist William Ferrel (1817–91), who identified them in 1856. The poleward-moving air produces low-altitude wind systems in middle latitudes called *westerlies.* This moderately warm air ascends at about latitude 60° and diverges at the tropopause, with part flowing equatorward to complete the circuit of Hadley cells and part continuing poleward in the upper troposphere.

Ferrel cells are generated by the interaction between Hadley cells and a third type of cell, *polar cells.* At the poles, cold, dense air descends from the tropopause to Earth's surface, creating a region of high pressure at low altitude. This cool air flows equatorward until it meets rising air from Ferrel cells at about 60° latitude. The polar air rises, gaining heat from rising air in the Ferrel cells, and then diverges at the tropopause, with some of the warm air moving poleward at high altitude, thus completing the circulation between latitudes 60° and 90°. In polar cells, cool air moving toward lower latitudes at low altitude and deflected by the Coriolis effect, form the winds called *polar easterlies.*

Where atmospheric cells meet, at about latitudes 30° and 60°, there is a sharp temperature difference across the boundary between one cell and the other. This difference creates strong airflows, called *jet streams,* that blow from west to east in the upper troposphere at altitudes of 30,000–50,000 feet (9,460–15,235 m) as high-altitude westerlies. Subtropical jet streams tend to be fairly constant throughout the year. Polar front jet streams—those produced between Ferrel and polar cells—tend to be both stronger and more variable. In winter, the polar front jet stream blows at 150–300 mph (241–483 km/h) and occasionally becomes unstable, breaking up to produce *anticyclones* (air masses rotating around high-pressure centers) that can maintain cloudless skies and still, cold conditions at ground level for weeks on end. Earlier in the winter, the polar front moving south causes cold polar air to overlie warm, tropical air beneath, a situation that tends to trigger *depressions* (air masses rotating around low-pressure centers) that produce snowfalls.

Taiga regions lie between latitudes 45°N and 70°N, so their weather is shaped by the easterlies of polar cells, the westerlies of Ferrel cells, and the polar jet stream associated with their boundary. The polar front (the boundary between polar and Ferrel cells) pushes farther south in winter and shifts farther north in summer, roughly defining the northern and southern limits of the taiga zone in North America (see sidebar).

## The changing seasons

The Earth spins once on its axis every 24 hours. When a location on Earth's surface is facing the Sun, it experiences daytime, and when it is turned away, it experiences nighttime. The seasons occur because the Earth is tilted on its spinning axis. During the summer in the Northern Hemisphere, the North Pole is tilted toward the Sun, the Sun reaches higher in

## North American taiga and the polar front

In North America, air masses, ocean currents, and land barriers combine to make the polar front—the boundary between tropical air masses moving north and polar air masses moving south—relatively stable. As a result, there is an unusually close agreement between the positions of the taiga and that of the polar front. The taiga-tundra boundary coincides approximately with the average position of the polar front in summer. The taiga's southern limit roughly corresponds with the polar front's average position in winter.

the sky, and the days are longer and warmer. During the Northern Hemisphere winter, the North Pole is tilted away from the Sun, the Sun is low in the sky, and the days are shorter and cooler. At the spring and autumn equinox, in March and September, the 24-hour span is divided equally into night and day.

The distribution of winds and weather, powered by the Sun, shifts with the season. In winter, wind and weather patterns penetrate farthest south. The weather in taiga regions is

*Seasons in the Northern Hemisphere*

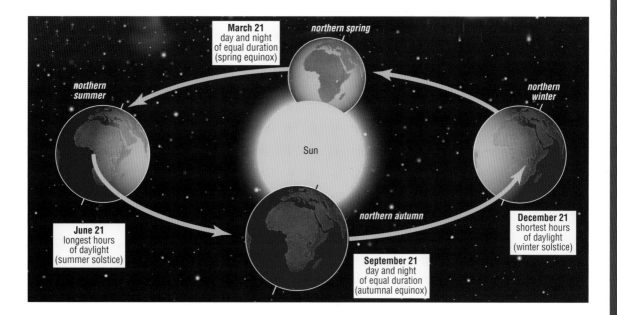

**March 21** day and night of equal duration (spring equinox)

*northern spring*

*northern summer*

*northern winter*

Sun

**June 21** longest hours of daylight (summer solstice)

*northern autumn*

**December 21** shortest hours of daylight (winter solstice)

**September 21** day and night of equal duration (autumnal equinox) strongly influenced by air masses from polar regions. In summer, wind and weather patterns shift northward. Then, taiga regions become influenced by air masses originating in tropical regions. Because taiga is located at fairly high latitudes, the difference in hours of sunlight between summer and winter is large. In most of Alaska, for example, the longest day (the summer solstice) has well over 20 hours of daylight, while the shortest day (the winter solstice) has less than four hours. The Sun is low in the sky all year round, rising to only 49.5° above the horizon (its highest elevation) at the summer solstice.

## Air masses

The climate and weather of taiga regions, like those of other regions on Earth, are determined by *air masses*. An air mass is a region of air that has been influenced by the land or water it is moving across for long enough to have recognizable characteristics, such as a particular temperature range and humidity. Air masses that are influenced by landmasses are called continental (c), and those that form over the ocean are maritime (m). The dance of these air masses gives us the weather and climate we experience.

Water has an exceptionally high *specific heat capacity*. This means that it absorbs large amounts of heat energy before it warms appreciably—evident to anyone who has heated cold water to boiling point to hard-boil an egg. Water stores large quantities of heat and is also slow to release its heat when it cools. This combination of properties means that water acts as a heat store and a "heat buffer"—slow to warm, slow to cool, and moderating the temperature of its surroundings. In comparison, the land warms and cools more rapidly than the oceans and, of course, it contains much less water. Such characteristics affect the nature of continental air masses.

Continental air masses are drier than maritime year-round. In winter, the continental landmass is usually cooler than the nearby ocean (because landmasses cool more rapidly), so continental air masses are cold as well as dry. In summer, the continent tends to be warmer than nearby sea-

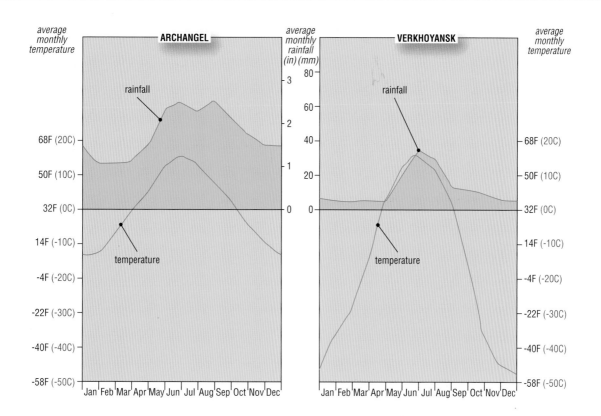

water (because landmasses heat more rapidly), so for a given latitude its air masses are likely to be hot as well as dry. As a general rule, the climate in the center of a continent is drier and has a more extreme difference between summer and winter temperatures than coastal areas at the same latitude. Archangel, in European Russia at about 65°N, has a maritime climate, while Verkhoyansk, eastern Siberia, at about 68°N, has a continental climate. The climographs above show the average monthly temperature and rainfall at each location. Notice how the annual temperature range at Verkhoyansk is greater than that of Archangel and its rainfall so much less.

Air masses are also named after the latitudes in which they form. North America, for example, is influenced by four main types of air mass: cool, dry continental polar (cP); cool, wet maritime polar (mP); hot, dry continental tropical (cT); and hot, wet maritime tropical (mT).

*Climographs (climate summary charts) for Archangel, European Russia, and Verkhoyansk, eastern Siberia*

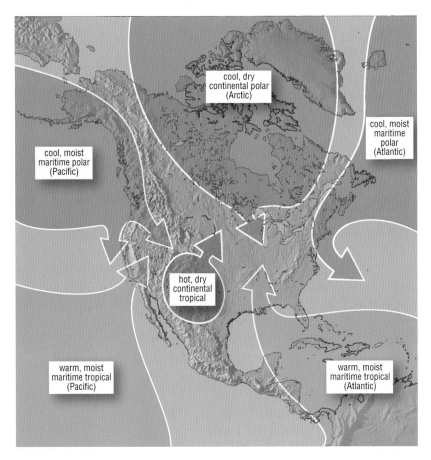

*North America's
air masses*

In central Canada in fall, cP air moves south, bringing cool, dry wintry weather, with warm air masses from the Gulf of Mexico only occasionally intruding. In summer, fair weather is punctuated with stormy conditions as the two air masses—dry air from Canada's west and northwest and humid air from the American South and Southwest—ebb and flow across North America. At the boundary, or *front,* between the two air masses, spectacular thunderstorms can develop when warm, moist air from near the ground rises into the colder air above. As the rising air cools, it unloads its moisture, which condenses to form rain droplets or ice crystals in dark cumulonimbus clouds (thunderclouds). In coastal New England in early spring, mP air masses from the northwest Atlantic bring fog and daytime temperatures often well below 50°F (10°C).

## The effect of the Great Lakes

The Great Lakes—because of their combined large size—act like a sea to moderate local temperatures and increase rainfall. Thus, Ontario has an unusual climate for a region in the heart of a continent. In mid-summer, cool breezes blowing off the Great Lakes may trigger fierce storms as they meet warmer air overland. In winter, the lakes seed the air with moisture, triggering blizzards to the west of the Great Lakes.

## Ocean currents and taiga

Ocean currents—often described as rivers in the sea—play a major role in transporting heat from the equator toward the poles. The currents themselves are mainly driven by the prevailing winds, such as the westerlies of mid-latitudes. But as water moves north or south, its motion is influenced by the Coriolis effect, which causes the current to turn. As a result, the main systems of currents in ocean basins tend to form circular systems, called *gyres*. In the Northern Hemisphere, the current systems within mid-latitude gyres flow clockwise. At higher latitudes, mini-gyres flowing in the opposite direction—counterclockwise—bring cooler water from polar regions to feed the mid-latitude gyres.

At the latitudes where taiga is established, cool currents flowing southward chill the air in coastal regions. This effect tends to extend taiga farther south in coastal regions than in the continental interior (see the map on page 5). The conspicuous exception is northwest Europe. Far from being chilled by cool, southward-flowing ocean currents, this region is warmed by the Gulf Stream and its northerly extension, the North Atlantic Drift. The North Atlantic Drift warms the air of coastal regions in northwest Europe and displaces the southern boundary of the taiga farther north.

The effects of the North Atlantic Drift are dramatic but not unchangeable. Climatologists are concerned that should global warming continue, it is feasible that the North Atlantic Drift might cease to break away from the mid-latitude gyre (see "Global warming and the taiga," pages 55–58). Deprived of its warm ocean current, northwest Europe would be plunged into climatic conditions at least 10°F (6°C) cooler, on average, than today. It sounds paradoxical that global warming should create a cooling effect, but the present route of the North Atlantic Drift is maintained by chilled seawater descending to the sea bottom to form North Atlantic Deep Water (NADW) beneath the edge of the Arctic ice. Surface water flows across from the North Atlantic Drift to replace this water. Should global warming prevent the formation of NADW, then the North Atlantic Drift might fail. This is not as far-fetched as it sounds.

Scientists examining the remains of zooplankton (animal plankton) in the sediments at the bottom of the North Atlantic have discovered layers containing cold-water species sandwiched between layers containing warm-water forms. It appears that about 11,000 years ago the NADW was disrupted, and cool-water zooplankton thrived in northeast Atlantic waters where warm-water plankton live today. At that time, the last (Devensian) glaciation was subsiding and ice sheets were shrinking. The melting Laurentide ice sheet covering much of North America was adding cold freshwater to the North Atlantic Drift, and the polar front had shifted northward as far as Iceland. The combined effects of these two events was sufficient to temporarily disrupt the formation of NADW and to cause the North Atlantic Drift to fail. In the midst of an overall global warming trend, northwest Europe was plunged into ice-age conditions for above 1,000 years, a climatic reversal called the Younger Dryas. Human-induced global warming could have a similar effect, and scientists are seeking to computer model the likelihood of this occurring in this millennium.

## Snow

In mid- and upper latitudes of the world, snow falls when water droplets in clouds coalesce around ice crystals. The ice crystals grow into snowflakes, and when they reach sufficient volume and mass, the snowflakes fall out of the cloud, attracted by Earth's gravitational pull. Should air temperatures below the cloud rise above the freezing point of water at that air pressure, then the falling snowflakes will melt into rain before reaching Earth's surface. If the snowflakes do not melt or evaporate during their fall, then they will reach Earth's surface still frozen, and if the ground temperature is close to or below freezing, they will settle. In many parts of the world's taiga, snow falls in September and remains as a covering layer over ground and vegetation for at least six months.

The snow has a beneficial effect for many plants and ground-living animals. Being pale, the snow reflects sunlight, so it does not readily absorb the Sun's heat energy and melt as it would if it were darker. Snow contains trapped air that is a poor heat conductor, so snow forms an insulating layer. It helps keep the soil warm in winter, protected from the chilly air, and it reduces temperature fluctuations. In mid-winter, the soil at a depth of 20 inches (50 cm) is typically at least 27°F (15°C) warmer than air temperature. Remove the layer

*The thick layer of snow that covers the ground in winter insulates small plants and ground-living animals from the chilly air temperatures above.* (Courtesy of Konrad Wothe/Minden Pictures)

## Taiga blizzards

In many parts of the taiga, snow blizzards (snow driven by high winds) are uncommon. This is because high winds and the two factors that cause moisture to crystallize as snow—cool temperatures and moist air—rarely coincide. However, in parts of the Siberian taiga, snow blizzards can be a deadly feature. A blizzard locally called the buran carries continental polar air from the northeast traveling behind a depression (a rotating air mass in which the air pressure decreases to a minimum at the center). It unloads snow and soon builds to hurricane force (wind speeds greater than 74 mph; 120 km/h), throwing settled snow into the air and creating almost zero visibility.

of snow, and the ground temperature plummets, making the surface soil likely to freeze solid. Some taiga plants have specific adaptations to prevent them from freezing, even without an insulating blanket of snow (see sidebar), but many cannot survive the depths of winter without a covering of snow to protect them.

In conclusion, taiga has a subarctic or cold temperate climate, with long cold winters and short summers ranging from cool to warm. Polar air masses dominate the taiga for much of the year, with northward-moving fronts in summer typically bringing at least half of the annual precipitation. In the center of North American and Eurasian continental landmasses, well away from the moderating effect of the sea, the

## Surviving supercooling

Pure water freezes at 32°F (0°C), but some larch trees can tolerate air temperatures of −76°F (−60°C), so surely the trees must be frozen solid? It appears this is not the case. During the winter, the larch loses water, and sugars and other substances become concentrated in its tissues. High concentrations of dissolved substances lower the freezing point of the tree's remaining water. This helps to prevent the tree's fluids from developing ice crystals that would damage its tissues.

temperature difference between summer and winter is extreme. Overall, average annual precipitation in the taiga is usually quite low (15–20 inches; 38–50 cm), but with cool temperatures and hence low rates of evaporation, this is sufficient to sustain tree growth.

## Taiga advance and retreat

Research carried out over the last 30 years suggests that the boreal forest has been on the move, back and forth, over many thousands of years. The taiga zone has migrated south during ice ages, or *glacials*—periods in Earth's recent geological history when ice sheets and glaciers were extensive. It has then moved north during milder periods, or *interglacials*, such as the current interglacial, the Flandrian, which has lasted some 12,000 years to the present. About 5,000 years ago, the global climate began to cool very slightly, halting and slightly reversing the northward advance of the taiga. In parts of Canada and Siberia, taiga's northern limit moved southward by 60–120 miles (100–200 km) between about 3000 B.C.E. and 1900 C.E. Since then, a slight global warming may be causing the taiga to migrate slightly northward again (see "Global warming and the taiga," pages 55–58).

The clues for this advance and retreat come from fossilized parts of plants and from ice cores that record the Earth's past temperatures and the ancient composition of its air. For example, scientists compare modern forests and the records of pollen they leave behind with tree pollen preserved in lake sediments thousands of years ago. Tracing these pollen records over time, scientists can piece together how the distribution of North American vegetation has changed since the end of the last glacial maximum, some 20,000 years ago.

At that time, an ice sheet called the Laurentide covered about half of North America, including almost all of Canada, to a depth of up to two miles (3.2 km). North America's vegetation was squeezed southward. At that time, spruce trees were widespread in the central United States, and they even reached as far south as Texas. Today most of this landscape is much too warm and dry to support spruce.

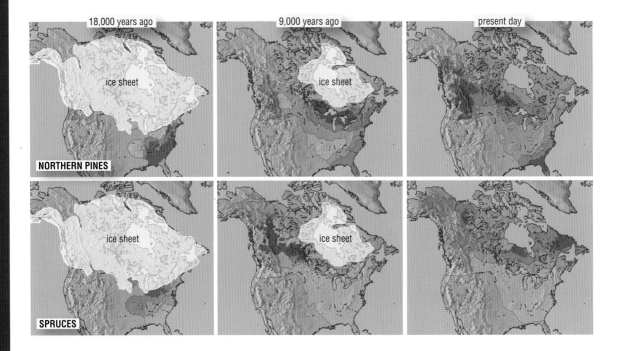

18,000 years ago   9,000 years ago   present day

NORTHERN PINES

SPRUCES

*The northward advance of North American pine and spruce trees in the last 18,000 years. As temperatures have risen and the Laurentide ice sheet has shrunk, conifer trees have migrated northward. The tree distributions are shown in red or pink according to the density of tree growth.*

Those North American coniferous forests that existed 20,000 years ago not only lay much farther south than they do today, but they were nowhere near as dense. The climate at that time appears to have been both cold and dry—not conducive to the growth of dense forest. Boreal forest as we know it today was probably restricted to low-lying land in the vicinity of lakes, rivers, and other sources of water.

When the Laurentide ice sheet began to retreat slowly northward some 18,000 years ago, tundra plants, such as tough grasses and heather, and then taiga trees, such as spruce and northern pine species, followed in its wake. By 15,000 years ago, the northern limit for these conifers reached almost as far as Newfoundland. Fir and birch trees generally require more moisture than spruce, and they followed the northward migration several thousand years later. Between 12,000 and 9,000 years ago, North America's climate grew milder and probably wetter, although cold spells lasting at least hundreds of years still punctuated the trend. Some 9,000 years ago, the boreal forests of southeast Canada close to the receding edge of the ice sheet were dominated by northern pine species. The preponderance of pine probably indicates that summer temperatures were too warm to favor spruce. Since, then, the boreal forest has not simply moved north as the ice has receded. The mix of species in the forest has changed too. Spruce, for example, has become much more widespread across Canada.

Looking to the future based on our knowledge of the past, if global warming causes a change in the distribution of boreal forest, we can expect a change in the balance of taiga tree species. And with that, we can expect a shift in the balance of the rest of the taiga plant and animal community as well.

## Global warming and the taiga

In the 1990s, the average annual temperatures in the Northern Hemisphere were the highest since detailed climatic records began to be compiled in the first half of the 19th century. This could be a sign of global warming, a trend showing a rise in average temperatures across the globe. Global warming is too complex and slow a process for many scientists to be readily convinced that it is actually happening, and if it is, what is the best way to combat it (see "Climate change," pages 161–163). Assessing whether global warming is taking place depends on decades of measurements to ensure that any rise is not just a temporary anomaly. Global climate is the sum total of regional climates across the globe. Even if some regions are becoming warmer, others are becoming cooler as climate patterns shift. It is necessary to work out average temperatures across the globe, month by month, year by year, to see whether there is a trend.

The Intergovernmental Panel on Climate Change (IPCC), a group made up of hundreds of scientists from across the globe, has been meeting regularly since 1990 to evaluate whether global warming is taking place and, if it is, what is the cause and what can be done about it. On balance, the IPCC is convinced that global warming is taking place and that rising levels of greenhouse gases in the atmosphere are the most likely cause.

Meanwhile, measurements using remote-sensing satellites suggest that since the 1980s, trees in the taiga belt have been photosynthesizing more than before. This could be a good thing because photosynthesizing plants remove carbon dioxide from the air. Currently, carbon dioxide levels in the global atmosphere are increasing, probably caused by humans burning more fossil fuels. Carbon dioxide is a greenhouse gas implicated in global warming (see sidebar). Any natural process that slows, halts, or reverses rising atmospheric carbon dioxide levels might help counter global warming.

Scientists are currently investigating whether the taiga is photosynthesizing more because average annual temperatures at Earth's surface are rising. If so, warmer temperatures could be causing the tree cover to shift northward, increasing the total area of cover, or it could be that higher spring temperatures permit existing trees to start photosynthesizing earlier in the season. Or both processes might be involved, in which case the taiga might be the biggest part of the *Great Northern Sink*. This is the term scientists use to refer to Northern Hemisphere organisms that play a major role in remov-

*The greenhouse effect*

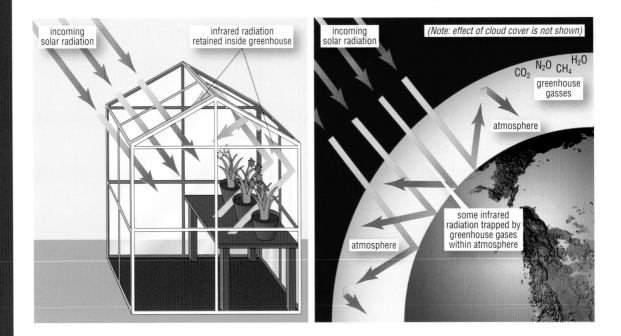

## The greenhouse effect

The greenhouse effect is a natural feature of Earth's atmosphere that has been operating for billions of years. It is caused by certain atmospheric gases—dubbed "greenhouse gases"—most notably water vapor, carbon dioxide, and methane.

When sunlight strikes the Earth's surface, some of the absorbed energy is emitted back into space as infrared radiation. Greenhouse gases absorb some of the outgoing infrared radiation, thus trapping heat in the atmosphere. During Earth's history, the greenhouse effect has been vital in sustaining a rich variety of life on Earth. Without the greenhouse effect, the planet would probably be, on average, at least 54°F (30°C) cooler than it is.

The name "greenhouse effect" comes from the superficial similarity between the operation of greenhouse gases and the glass in a greenhouse. On a sunny day in winter, the inside of a greenhouse is noticeably warmer than the air outside. The effect is due to the greenhouse glass, which helps prevent infrared radiation leaving the greenhouse and so has a pronounced warming effect.

The problem with the atmospheric greenhouse effect is not that it is happening, but that human activities appear to be "enhancing" the natural greenhouse effect. Globally, people are burning more fossil fuels—in particular, petroleum oil products, coal, and natural gas—than ever before. This activity is releasing additional carbon dioxide into the atmosphere that is enhancing the greenhouse effect, trapping more heat energy in the atmosphere and contributing to global warming.

ing carbon dioxide from the air. A "sink" is a store or surplus. In this case, it is a store of carbon.

No link between the taiga, greenhouse gases, and global warming is straightforward. Even if the taiga is photosynthesizing more and thus helping to reduce atmospheric carbon dioxide levels, which might combat global warming, other processes are also at work. For example, as the planet warms, tundra and taiga are likely to shift location, and their relative abundances are likely to change too. These biomes differ in their reflectiveness to light (albedo), and changes in their relative abundance would influence global warming in subtle ways.

On average, snow-covered tundra reflects nearly 70 percent of sunlight while snow-covered taiga reflects about 50 percent (the dark branches absorb more sunlight than the pale snow). Put another way, an acre of winter taiga absorbs more sunlight than an acre of winter tundra. If the area of taiga increases at the expense of tundra, this could have a winter warming effect because of increased sunlight absorption. On the other hand, removing part of the taiga forest should reduce the amount of photosynthesis—at least temporarily—which would lessen the uptake of the greenhouse gas carbon dioxide from the air. From a global warming point of view this would seem to be a bad thing. However, a cleared patch of ground that is covered in snow is more reflective than the snow-covered trees that once grew there. The bare ground could have a local cooling effect in winter. Thus, the effect on global warming of increasing or decreasing the global area of taiga forest is far from clear. What is apparent is that the checks and balances that affect global warming are complex and, as yet, not well understood.

# CHAPTER 4

# TAIGA BIOLOGY

Standing in the taiga and looking around, a person will see more than anything else trees, but not the dozen or more species they might find in broad-leaved forests in temperate climates farther south. In taiga, one or two tree species usually dominate the forest, and they are conifers. It is only in clearings in the forest that a wide variety of trees—including broad-leaved trees—maintain a foothold.

## Dark or light taiga?

The densest taiga forests are called *dark taiga.* They are called this not so much because the trees grow so closely together that their canopies of branches and leaves cut out most of the sunlight—which they do—but because the trees tend to have dark leaves. Spruce and fir trees dominate the dark taiga. One way to tell them apart is to examine their ripe cones. In firs, cones grow upright, above the branch. In spruces, the cones start upright, but as they ripen they come to hang down beneath the branch. The exception to the rule is the Douglas fir that, like the spruce, has ripe cones that hang down.

Dark taiga exists where soil and climatic conditions are not too extreme. Where the climate is dry and cold, and the soil lacking in nutrients, *light taiga* (conifers with lighter leaves) tends to dominate. This is also the case where ground fires are frequent.

Pines and larches dominate light taiga. They generally have paler leaves than spruces and firs. Larch cones grow singly and upright, above the branch. In light taiga, a tree with cones hanging beneath the branch is likely to be a pine.

## Dark conifers

The spruces (genus *Picea*) are the most common conifers of the dark taiga. In European forests, the Norway spruce (*Picea*

# What is a cone?

The cone is the conifer's answer to a flower. It contains the structures involved in sexual reproduction. Cones form on the branches of mature conifers, with male cones normally maturing in a single season and female cones over two or more. Male cones, typically smaller and softer than female cones, produce pollen grains that contain male sex cells. The pollen is carried on the wind to reach female cones of the same species. When male sex cells in pollen fuse with female sex cells in the female cone, the combination produces seeds. Once seeds begin to form, the woody scales on the female cone close, protecting the developing seeds inside until they are ripe and ready to be released. The scales then bend outward to scatter the ripe seeds on the wind. This usually happens in fall, but in the case of pines, the ripe seeds are usually released the following spring.

Given the right conditions, the seeds germinate and grow into adult plants of the next generation. In some cases, animals help in seed dispersal by swallowing seeds that pass through the gut intact or transporting ones that are entangled in the animal's fur or feathers (see "Pollination and seed dispersal," pages 71–72).

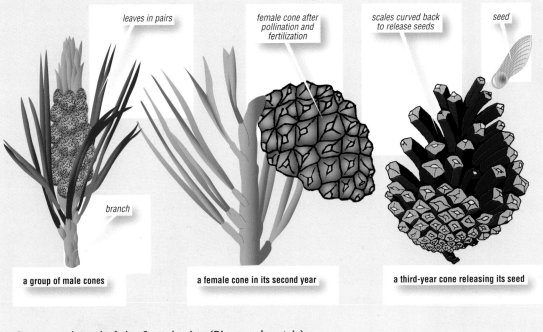

leaves in pairs

female cone after pollination and fertilization

scales curved back to release seeds

seed

branch

a group of male cones

a female cone in its second year

a third-year cone releasing its seed

*Cones and seed of the Scotch pine* (Pinus sylvestris)

*abies*) is the dominant species. In Siberia, the Siberian spruce (*Picea obovata*) replaces it, with Siberian spruce and yeddo spruce (*Picea jezoensis*) common in parts of Ussuriland.

The spruces of Europe and Asia need damp but not water-logged soil throughout the year. They are slow growing, but under favorable conditions they cover vast areas of taiga. Old-growth spruce forests are dark and cool at ground level, with the ground littered with decaying fallen branches and tree trunks. These brooding forests have spawned stories of trolls, gnomes, and wood-goblins in Nordic folklore. Eurasian spruce forests are at their most attractive in winter when snow covers the ground and branches, lightening the scene.

In North America, white or black spruces dominate the dark taiga. The white spruce (*Picea glauca*) needs similar growing conditions to those of Eurasian spruces. It is a tall, elegant conifer reaching 150 feet (45 m) high with a pointed crown, and specimens live up to 600 years. The black (or bog) spruce (*Picea mariana*), on the other hand, is rather small and unattractive in comparison. It often reaches only about 40 feet (12 m) high and has a slender, slightly crooked trunk and a tufted crown looking rather like an upended broom. The black spruce is at a competitive advantage in areas with cooler, damper ground. It is more common above permafrost and in boggy areas.

Fir trees (genus *Abies*) demand milder conditions, more moisture, and more fertile soils than spruces require, so they do not grow as far north as spruces or as high up mountains. In Asia, the Siberian fir (*Abies sibirica*) grows among Siberian spruces, and the Siberian white fir (*Abies nephrolepsis*) grows mixed in with yeddo spruce. The silver fir (*Abies alba*), the most widespread fir in Europe, does not grow in the main taiga zone but is widespread on lower mountain slopes to the south.

In North America, firs inhabit mountainous regions and penetrate farther south than spruces. The balsam fir (*Abies balsamea*)—a small tree that yields Canada balsam, a resin used for mounting biological or medical specimens on microscope slides—is widespread in the main taiga zone. The Douglas fir (*Pseudotsuga menziesii*), one of the world's largest trees at up to 330 feet (100 m) high with a trunk 16 feet (5 m) in diameter, is found in small numbers in the main taiga zone. It forms forests in the Rocky Mountains and is common in the mixed conifer and broad-leaved forests of North America's Pacific coast.

## Light conifers

Light conifers of the taiga—pines and larches—are more widely distributed than dark conifers because they can tolerate a broader range of environmental conditions. Some larches (genus *Larix*) survive the temperature extremes of the driest and coldest continental taiga, while pine species (genus *Pinus*) survive in dry, infertile, sandy soils that cannot support spruces. In fact, the best growing conditions for spruces and pines are similar, but spruces tend to outcompete pines in the long run unless environmental conditions are regularly disturbed by factors such as pest attacks or fires. Pines tend to become displaced into environmental conditions that are more hostile to spruces.

The Scotch pine (*Pinus sylvestris*) is the most widespread light conifer in Europe. The Siberian pine (*Pinus sibirica*), actually called a dark conifer, because of its dark foliage, replaces the Scotch pine in the forests of central and eastern Siberia. It rarely grows in single-species stands, but is usually mixed with larch or birch. The Korean pine (*Pinus koraiensis*), another dark conifer, grows in the Far East taiga.

The unusual dwarf Siberian pine (*Pinus pumila*) grows to only 16 feet (5 m) tall as a shrub. In its habitat in the mountains of eastern Siberia and Far East Asia, its tangle of branches traps a thick layer of snow that insulates and protects it during the cold winters.

In North America, the jack pine (*Pinus banksiana*) is a common light conifer of the main taiga belt. It outcompetes spruce under similar conditions to those of the Scotch pine in Europe, namely in sandy soils and in places where the tree cover is periodically cleared by natural forces or human action.

Another common light conifer is the ponderosa pine (*Pinus ponderosa*), but it favors locations south of the main taiga belt. It is the famous pine of the Rocky Mountains, forming a common backdrop in western movies and television series. It grows at sea level in Washington State and at altitudes as high as 9,850 feet (3,000 m) in Arizona.

The larches are light conifers that shed their leaves in winter. These hardy trees survive farther north than any other conifer. They are similar to pines in their competitive abilities in relation to spruces, but they are more cold resistant than pines.

In North America, the tamarack (*Larix laricina*) is the most widespread larch. It grows in parts of Alaska and most of Canada. The western larch (*Larix occidentalis*) grows immensely tall, as high as 260 feet (80 m), in stands north of the Rocky Mountains. It forms large, economically productive forests that are maintained by periodic ground fires that prevent spruce from establishing themselves.

In Eurasian taiga, the Siberian larch (*Larix sibirica*) is found in northern Europe and the Daurian larch (*Larix gmelinii*) in central and eastern Siberia, as well as in parts of Mongolia and northeast China. Almost half of Russian taiga forest is larch forest. The Kamchatka larch (*Larix kamtschatica*) is the native species of the Far East taiga, extending from Kamchatka southward to parts of Japan.

## Broad-leaved trees of the taiga

Birches (genus *Betula*), aspens, and poplars (genus *Populus*) are the most common broad-leaved trees of the taiga. They are members of the group of flowering plants (the class Angiospermae). Plants that produce flowers have some advantages over cone-bearing plants. Flowers can be brightly colored and richly scented to attract insects that carry pollen from one flower to another. Flowering plants also produce seeds enclosed in fruits. Fruits can offer additional protection, as in the case of trees bearing hard nuts. Or they can assist in seed dispersal, as with succulent fruits that are consumed by animals, with the seeds passing through the animals' digestive system unharmed.

However, broad-leaved trees shed their leaves in winter, and in many taiga situations, they are at a competitive disadvantage compared with conifers. As a general rule, broad-leaved

*Birch trees (genus Betula) in Sunlit Grove, Superior National Forest, Minnesota. They are one of the few types of deciduous trees that flourish in parts of the taiga.* (Courtesy of Jim Brandenburg/ Minden Pictures)

trees require more light and more fertile soils than conifers. Because they have to grow new leaves each year, there is a delay before they can photosynthesize in early summer, so the growing season of broad-leaved trees is short in taiga regions. However, in Europe, silver birch (*Betula pendula*) and trembling aspen (*Populus tremula*)—both broad-leaved tree species—are often the first trees to colonize a clearing in taiga forest, before conifers outcompete them. In North America, the paper birch (*Betula papyrifera*) and trembling aspen (*Populus tremuloides*) are successful early colonizers. Trembling aspens get their name from the shaking effect of the wind rustling their leaves.

In the milder conditions found in southern taiga forests, birches and aspens grow scattered among the conifers. The Siberian poplar (*Populus suaveolens*) in Eurasia and the balsam poplar (*Populus balsamifera*) in North America form dense stands where taiga rivers lay down sediment deposits around their banks, producing fertile soil. Conifers usually replace these poplars after a few decades.

## Beneath the canopy

Whether in light or dark taiga, the tree canopy is usually dense enough to cut out most of the sunlight reaching the forest floor. Only shade-tolerant plants can survive in the gloom. At the same time, tree roots capture most of the water and nutrients in the soil, so shrubs and nonwoody plants need to be tolerant of nutrient-poor conditions on the forest floor. Coupled with this is the problem of coniferous leaf litter—the needles that fall from conifer trees. These smother young plants and also release toxic substances. Where taiga is dense, no ground-level plants may grow at all. Only in clearings or in less dense woodland do a wide variety of plants grow on the forest floor. However, natural fires, waterlogged soil, the ravages of wood- or leaf-eating insects, and other factors ensure that parts of the forest have clearings or thin conifer cover, and these openings provide opportunities for other plants to grow. Such places are refuges from which seeds can disperse to germinate in any fresh clearings.

*Vegetation layers in the taiga forest*

Plants grow at various levels beneath the tree canopy. In the canopy and below some plants grow on the trees themselves. Unlike the trees of tropical rain forests, which are festooned with climbing plants, taiga conifers harbor almost none, just a few species of the flowering plant *Clematis*. However simpler plants—algae, lichens, and mosses—can grow in abundance on branches and parts of the tree trunk (see "Mosses and lichens," pages 69–71). These plants are called *epiphytes* (from *epi,* meaning "upon," and *phyton,* meaning "plant"). They grow on the surface of other plants but do not gain their food supplies from them.

Smaller epiphytes tend to be particularly sensitive to air pollution, and the type and abundance of epiphytes on taiga trees are indicators of air quality. Other factors aside, the cleaner the air, the wider variety of epiphytes. Lichens—a strange partnership between algae and fungi—are one group of epiphytes. They are *symbiotic,* meaning they form a close association between individuals of very different species. Fruticose lichens, which look like miniature shrubs, are particularly sensitive to air pollution. They are the first to succumb when levels of sulfur dioxide released by the burning of "dirty" fossil fuels, such as sulfur-rich fuel oil or coal, increase in the vicinity (see "Air pollution," pages 153–158). Scientists record the types, abundance, and condition of lichens as a quick way of assessing local air quality. If the air is heavily polluted, epiphytic lichens may be totally absent.

A shrub layer grows on the forest floor to a height of about 13 feet (4 m) where typically there are moderate light levels. The shrub layer tends to be most pronounced in the southern taiga. Alders, wild roses, junipers, raspberries, and honeysuckles are among the shrubs that grow on the forest floor. Their tangled branches and shoots provide a haven for forest animals, which can hide there or, in the case of some birds and mammals, make their nests there. The fruits of berry-laden shrubs offer a rich food source.

One of these taiga shrubs, the alder (genus *Alnus*), bases its success on a long-standing symbiotic partnership. The roots of alders harbor fungi that grow in outgrowths called nodules. The fungi trap or "fix" nitrogen from the air—something that very few organisms can do. Nitrogen is a nutrient all plants require to manufacture carbon-based substances, such as proteins and nucleic acids, which contain nitrogen. Most plants acquire nitrogen in the form of nitrates dissolved in soil water. Alder can obtain its nitrate supply from its nitrogen-fixing fungal partners, so the shrub can thrive in nitrate-deficient soils. In exchange, the alder provides the fungus with a secure home.

Beneath the shrub layer is a layer of *herbaceous* plants (flowering plants without woody stems) that reach up to about two feet (60 cm) above the forest floor. They include the twinflower, starflower, May lily, and common wood sorrel. In this layer also grow low-lying shrubs, such as bilberry and cowberry.

Shrubs and herbaceous plants often grow in patches on the forest floor, so that when scientists analyze the ground cover of the forest, they discover a patchwork or mosaic of different plants. This pattern comes about usually by opportunistic colonization. If a clearing becomes available, the first seeds to arrive and germinate can establish themselves and overshadow competitors that arrive later (see the sidebar, "Death

## Death of a tree

A falling tree gives an insight into how the taiga forest—seemingly fairly uniform—is actually made up of a patchwork of microenvironments that change over time. When a large tree falls over, its roots tear a crater in the ground. The soil attached to the tree roots, now unearthed and exposed to the air, is loose and well drained. For a short time, this situation offers excellent growing conditions for shrubs and nonwoody plants, with the gap in the canopy overhead letting in bright shafts of sunlight. Meanwhile, mosses, lichens, and fungi grow on the fallen trunk itself. Many studies have shown that conifer seeds fail to germinate on much of the forest floor because the thick layer of pine needles inhibits growth. But a fallen tree, as it rots, creates an ideal nursery for the seedlings of conifer trees. These conditions, favorable for a wide variety of plants, last only as long as the canopy remains open. Once one or more trees grow to fill the gap, the area around the fallen tree gradually becomes more like the rest of the dense forest once again.

of a tree"). Many herbaceous plants or shrubs can spread out across the ground by sending out *rhizomes* (horizontal, underground stems) or *stolons* (horizontal, aboveground stems). These establish new plants nearby, creating a single-species patch or clump.

Often hugging the ground lies a layer of mosses or lichens that grow directly on the soil surface. Mosses are more prevalent in the dark and damp of the forest. Lichens require more light and drier conditions, and they grow well in clearings and in the sandy soils of pine forests. In the open larch forests of eastern Siberia, mosses dominate the shadowed soil under trees while lichens thrive in the gaps in between.

Both mosses and lichens can survive seasonal desiccation (drying out). Lichens are faded, crisp, and fragile in the dry season, when they give the appearance of being dead. When wet weather returns, they swell and brighten and resume photosynthesis once more.

## Partners beneath the soil

A person endowed with Superman's finely tuned X-ray vision would see beneath the forest floor a tangled tracery of threads running through every inch of leaf litter, extending through the fertile regions of the soil, and even enveloping the roots of trees. This remarkable network is the hidden feeding system of soil fungi. Most fungi reveal themselves only when their fruiting bodies—mushrooms and toadstools—rise from the forest floor. The tangled web beneath the soil is the fungi's system of feeding tubes, called *hyphae*. Many of the soil fungi form *mycorrhizae*—intimate partnerships with trees.

Without mycorrhizae, boreal forests would be nowhere near as productive as they are. Cones and conifer needles are tough and resistant to decay, so they could take many years to break down under the action of bacteria and other decomposers in the cool of the taiga forest floor. Mycorrhizae speed up the decay process.

The hyphae of mycorrhizal fungi grow around conifer fragments in and on the soil. They release digestive enzymes that break down the plant matter. The fungi absorb the nutrients for their own needs but pass on some to tree roots through their complex network of hyphae. Some of the fungus's hyphae grow into the cells of tree roots and exchange substances with the tree. The tree benefits by having a supply of freshly recycled nutrients; the fungi's system of hyphae acts like an extension of the tree's root system. Some mycorrhizal fungi confer another benefit on trees: They produce antibiotics that kill or halt soil bacteria that might harm the tree. The mycorrhizal fungi benefit by having a regular supply of dead plant material provided by the tree. The tree also furnishes the fungi with sugars and vitamins that help the fungi grow.

## Mosses and lichens

The bryophytes are a group of simple plants, the mosses and liverworts. Mosses, though small, tend to be more upright,

*Reindeer moss* (Cladonia rangiferina) *is a type of lichen, not a moss. It is an important component in the winter diet of reindeer (caribou).* (Courtesy of Konrad Wothe/Minden Pictures)

while liverworts have ground-hugging leaflike structures. Mosses especially are important components of the damp taiga forest. They grow on the trunk and branches of trees as well as on the ground.

Like most other plants, mosses photosynthesize (trap sunlight to make food). But unlike vascular plants (plants such as ferns, conifers, and flowering plants, which have transporting tissues that act as a system of supports), mosses do not have leaves or leaflike structures containing veins. The lack of structured support and absence of specialized transporting tissues limit mosses to a small size. Also unlike vascular plants, mosses do not have true roots. Mosses take up water and nutrients from the soil using simpler structures called *rhizoids*. Mosses have an advantage over vascular plants in being able to absorb water and minerals directly from snow and rain—hence the ability of mosses to grow where there is little or no soil, such as on the bark of trees.

The disadvantages of the moss design restrict them to living in damp environments, although they can withstand drying out for part of the year. Many species of moss can lose more than two-thirds of their water content, drying out to become dormant, leathery tufts. They spring back to vibrant life when water returns. However, mosses do depend on plentiful water in the environment when they sexually reproduce. Male reproductive structures called *antheridia* release sperm that swim through water to reach the female reproductive structures, *archegonia,* on the same plant or other mosses of the same species. Conifers and flowering plants have an advantage over mosses because they produce pollen grains that resist drying out. Pollen are carried on the wind, or by insects, and do not require environmental water for successful transfer of the male gamete (sex cell). They do not depend on damp conditions, and their male sex cells can travel long distances compared to the free-swimming sperm cells of mosses.

Following successful fertilization in mosses, a structure called the *sporangium,* or capsule, grows from a stalk on the top of the moss plant. In dry weather, the capsule breaks open to release spores that settle and grow into new moss plants.

Lichens are unusual symbiotic partnerships between fungi and single-celled algae (very simple plants). Lichens grow on

## Sphagnum moss

The remarkable sphagnum mosses are the dominant plants in many bogs. They are extremely efficient at absorbing and retaining water. In damp hollows, sphagnum moss grows year after year on the remains of previous generations, so that the spongy thickness of partially decayed sphagnum, with a top layer of living moss, can reach many feet thick.

Sphagnum mosses bear dark capsules that burst open when ripe to fling spores several inches into the air. The spores germinate to grow into new sphagnum plants, but in many cases they depend upon the presence of symbiotic fungi to grow successfully.

the drier, more brightly lit parts of the forest floor; on the bark of trees; and on rock outcrops. Like mosses, lichens can dry out and become dormant, becoming active again when wetted.

The partners in lichen cannot survive without each other. They form an association that looks very different from either a fungus or a single-celled plant. The algal partner photosynthesizes and provides food for both. The fungal partner supplies both with water and minerals absorbed from rain and snow. The fungus also forms a protective sheath around its algae. In dry conditions, the sheath shrinks and closes, preventing water loss. When moisture returns, the sheath swells and opens, allowing the algae to photosynthesize once more.

Seen close up, the ground-living lichens form a miniature multicolored forest an inch or so tall, hugging the forest floor and covering moist bark and fallen branches. Lichens—looking like miniature shrubs—adorn many living tree branches. Some of the tree-growing lichens produce acids with antibacterial and antifungal properties. Some may even protect their host trees from attacks by wood-destroying microbes.

## Pollination and seed dispersal

Conifers are all wind-pollinated, as are most of the broadleaved trees of the taiga. The herbaceous (nonwoody) plants of the forest floor, on the other hand, are usually insect-pollinated. They bear flowers rich in nectar—a sugary secretion—that attracts insects. The insects inadvertently carry pollen from one flower to another, ensuring success-ful pollination. Starflowers, wintergreens, cowberries, the common wood sorrel, and the May lily have white flowers that show up well in the gloom of the forest to attract bees and butterflies. Some plants, such as the common wood sorrel and the May lily, can self-pollinate as well as cross-pollinate, increasing the options for successful sexual reproduction.

The summer season is short, and larger taiga animals are scarce, so small plants may have problems relying on animals to scatter fruits and seeds. As insurance against the failure of sexual reproduction, most taiga shrubs and small flowering plants can reproduce asexually (without the use of flowers) as well as sexually. They grow underground stems (rhizomes) or overground stems (stolons) that spread sideways and estab-lish the shoots and roots of new plants.

Taiga trees and shrubs produce fruits and seeds that form a major part of the diet of many resident animals. Many plants have evolved fruits that encourage birds and animals to con-sume them, so aiding the wide dispersal of the plant. Brown bears, stoats, squirrels, and capercaillie birds are among the wide range of taiga animals that consume the ripe berries of juniper, bilberry, and other shrubs. The seeds within the fruits often pass through the digestive system unharmed, and when the animal voids its waste, the seed is sown along with a helping of natural fertilizer.

Birds and animals also disperse seeds without actually con-suming them. The twinflower plant produces small, spiny fruit that catches in the fur or feathers of creatures that brush past. The seed, transported by animal, may not fall to the ground for many miles.

## Origins of the taiga animals

Many of the animal groups in North American taiga have the same or closely related species in Eurasian taiga. In the case of larger mammals, the same species are often found in both places, sometimes under different common names. Brown bears (*Ursus arctos*) and gray wolves (*Canis lupus*) are unevenly distributed across the taiga, from Alaska in the west to Siberia in the east. The North American wolverine is the same species (*Gulo gulo*) as the Eurasian glutton; the American caribou (*Rangifer tarandus*) is the Eurasian reindeer; and the moose is the elk (*Alces alces*). The occurrence of taiga species across so much of the taiga zone (including North America and Eurasia separated by the Atlantic and Pacific Oceans) is best explained by the geologically recent land links connecting the taiga region as a whole. Taiga animals originated in one or a few places and then spread to occupy much of the range before some of these land links disappeared.

Evidence from paleontology (the study of fossil remains) and genetics (the study of inherited characteristics) points to eastern Siberia about 500,000–600,000 years ago as the most likely place and time for the origin of many of today's taiga animals. At that time, eastern Siberia was covered in temperate broad-leaved forest. Since then, broad-leaved forests have given way to coniferous forests several times during the alternating glacial and interglacial periods that have followed. Meanwhile, taiga animals that evolved in eastern Siberia spread across the taiga biome, crossing into North America over the Bering land bridge connecting eastern Siberia with Alaska.

Regional differences in taiga animal species are usually best explained by an occasional influx of species from temperate or even tropical regions to the south. Thus, eastern Siberia has musk deer that originated in Southeast Asia. North American taiga contains rufous hummingbirds and striped skunks whose nearest living relatives are found in the tropical forests of South America.

## Taiga insects

A person visiting the taiga in summertime—particularly anywhere near standing water—cannot fail to meet buzzing, biting, flying insects. Near bogs and swamps, the air can be thick with blood-sucking mosquitoes, gnats, and blackflies.

Mosquitoes and gnats both belong to the insect family Culcidae and many favor the blood of mammals. Only the female mosquito is a bloodsucker. She pierces the skin of her victim with daggerlike parts of her mouth that enclose a sucking tube. She releases saliva into the wound to keep the blood flowing. Males, on the other hand, usually feast on the nectar of flowers.

The female mosquito needs her fill of fresh blood—often amounting to her own body weight—to provide the energy and nutrients for her eggs to mature. She lays them in almost any small patch of still water, and they hatch the following year, passing through several larval stages before becoming a *pupa,* the cased, nonfeeding developmental stage between larva and adult. The pupa splits open its casing at the water surface to liberate an adult mosquito.

Even more irritating than mosquitoes are tiny blackflies (family Simuliidae) less than a quarter-inch (6 mm) long. As with mosquitoes, female blackflies are bloodsuckers, needing blood for egg development, and they lay their eggs in water. Blackflies, however, require the flowing water of streams or rivers for egg-laying. The bite of the blackfly is painful. Dozens of bites can trigger an allergic reaction in the human victim, causing painful swelling and fever.

While some species of taiga insect attack large animals, many more attack trees. Others hunt, forage, or scavenge among the leaf litter on the forest floor.

Swarms of Siberian moths (*Dendrolimnus superans sibiricus*) gather on some midsummer evenings to lay their eggs on the needle leaves of conifers. The eggs hatch into miniature caterpillars that feed on the needles and then attack fresh shoots. Pine moths of the genus *Dioryctria* select those trees that are weakest—because of old age, previous disease, or unfavorable growing conditions. A tree attacked by hundreds of caterpillars becomes severely weakened. Other insects then attack the sickened tree, often killing it. The long-horned beetle, for example, lays eggs under conifer bark, and its grubs consume wood, undermining the strength of the tree trunk and causing the tree to collapse. From a broader perspective, this woodland damage is not all bad news. The accelerated death of weak trees creates gaps in the forest and opportunities for replacement by young trees (see the sidebar "Death of a tree," page 67).

In North America, the caterpillar of the spruce budworm moth (genus *Choristoneura*) plays a similar role to that of the pine moth caterpillar in ravaging weak trees. The budworm goes through a cycle of abundance: The insect peaks in some years, until parasites and predators curb their numbers; their numbers decline; and then the cycle repeats a few years later.

Grubs of the Cerambycidae family (long-horned beetles), which includes pine borers and sawyers as well as bark beetle grubs, cause wood destruction that fells trees. Some North American forestry experts recommend encouraging controlled attacks of bark beetle. They argue that controlled infestations thin the forest. This increases the range of habitats that, in turn, supports a richer biodiversity (see "Biodiversity," pages 169–172).

## Amphibians and reptiles

The taiga supports members of all four groups of land-living vertebrates (animals with backbones): amphibians, reptiles, birds, and mammals. Birds and mammals generate plentiful amounts of body heat and, except for those mammals that hibernate in winter, they maintain a fairly constant body temperature throughout the year. The body temperature of amphibians and reptiles, however, is largely governed by environmental temperature. They adjust their body temperature by behavioral means, such as basking in the sun to raise body temperature high enough so they can become active, or escaping into burrows to avoid temperature extremes. Few species of amphibian or reptile can survive the taiga's cold winters.

Remarkably, the Siberian salamander (*Salamandrella keyserlingii*), the most cold-adapted amphibian of taiga and tundra regions, can remain active at temperatures around the freezing point of water, which is 32°F (0°C). The salamander hibernates in winter and can survive underground beneath air temperatures as low as –31°F (–35°C).

The salamander spends most of the year on land and in the short summer, seeks out a small pool of water in which to mate. The male arrives first and releases attractant chemicals called *pheromones* into the water to entice females. Females release their eggs into the pond's weed beds, and the male fertilizes the eggs externally. The eggs hatch, and the emerging larvae grow in the water before leaving to find winter hideaways on land.

Temperatures in summer are so variable, with chilly spells always possible, that reptile eggs laid on the ground are unlikely to survive. Avoiding this hazard, the two common reptile species of European boreal forests, the lacertid lizard (*Lacerta vivipara*) and the European viper (*Vipera berus*), do not lay eggs but bear their young live as miniature versions of adults.

## Bird life

Roughly two-thirds of bird species that inhabit the taiga originated as passerines (perching birds) that evolved in temperate forests. Most of these birds migrate south from the taiga in winter and return in the summer.

For most bird species that overwinter in the taiga, the same or a closely related form occurs in both North America and Eurasia, as in the case of the North American black-capped chickadee (*Poecile atricapilla* formerly *Parus atricapillus*) and the Eurasian willow tit (*Poecile montana* formerly *Parus montanus*). On the other hand, among species that migrate south in winter, many in North America are not closely related to those in Eurasia. For example, some species of Old World warblers (family Sylviidae) and the New World warblers (Parulidae) have evolved to catch insects on conifer leaves. Being adapted to a similar lifestyle they resemble each other, but they are not closely related.

Woodpeckers (family Picidae), crossbills (genus *Loxia*), and nutcrackers (genus *Nucifraga*) are among the birds that remain in the taiga year-round. So, too, does the capercaillie of Eurasia (*Tetrao urogallus*), the largest taiga bird of all. The capercaillie, a type of grouse, can weigh 13 pounds (6 kg). It harvests wild fruits in summer and fall and subsists on a diet of pine needles in winter. In summer, males energetically defend their nesting territory against other males. A resident male will intimidate an intruding male by calling loudly and suddenly dropping to the ground from a tree branch. If the

*A chickadee, commonly called a "tit" in Eurasia (genus Poecile, formerly Parus), alighting on a conifer tree. Some species of chickadee remain in the taiga throughout the year.* (Courtesy of Michael Quinton/ Minden Pictures)

warning is not heeded, a fight may ensue. What starts off as ritualized fighting, in which one bird pretends to bite the other, can degenerate into a brawl, with one bird clasping the other's neck. Injury and death can result.

Among Eurasian woodpeckers, the black woodpecker (*Dryocopus martius*) is the biggest and loudest of all. It prefers old forests where it can excavate safe nesting holes in tall trees and where there is a plentiful supply of decaying wood that harbors its prey insects. With its chisel-like beak, the woodpecker hacks small holes on tree trunks and pries off bark to reveal the insects hidden beneath. Biologists have recorded the black woodpecker taking nearly 1,000 tree ants or wood-boring beetle grubs in a single meal.

The woodpecker's head conceals a remarkably long, pointed and barbed tongue that shoots out more than two inches (5 cm) to stab grubs or scoop up ants. The bird's skull has adaptations to prevent the bird inflicting damage upon itself with the vibrations from its wood-chiseling labors. A thick skull encloses fluid spaces and tough membranes that cushion the woodpecker's brain against physical shocks. Strong muscles also help absorb the thousands of wood-chiseling blows the woodpecker makes each day. So loud is the woodpecker's "ra-ta-tat" that it is audible more than a mile away.

*Beak size and cone preference in crossbills (genus Loxia)*

Wherever woodpeckers are found, their activities leave holes that hasten the decay of wood, as well as provide homes for other animals. Many creatures, including owls,

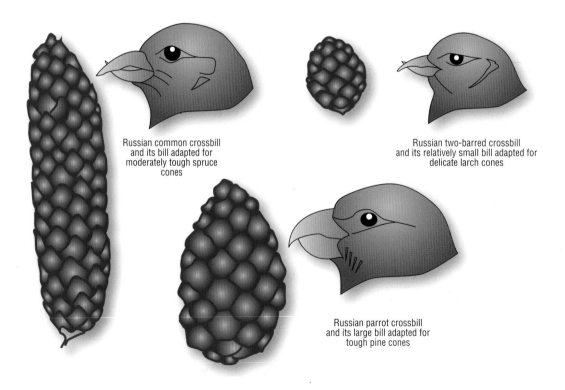

Russian common crossbill
and its bill adapted for
moderately tough spruce
cones

Russian two-barred crossbill
and its relatively small bill adapted for
delicate larch cones

Russian parrot crossbill
and its large bill adapted for
tough pine cones

pine martens, and squirrels, roost or nest in the discarded holes of woodpeckers.

Nutcrackers and crossbills subsist on the seeds of conifers. The two groups of birds have very different strategies for extracting seeds. Nutcrackers use a powerful beak to stab or batter spruce and pine cones to release the seeds. Crossbills, on the other hand, delicately pry open cone scales to reveal the seeds beneath. In a given region, different crossbill species are adapted to cope with cones of different shapes and sizes. In Siberian taiga, the parrot crossbill (*Loxia pytyopsittacus*) has a thick, rounded bill for opening robust pinecones. The common crossbill (*Loxia curvirostra*) has a medium-size bill adapted for spruce cones and softer pinecones. The two-barred crossbill (*Loxia leucoptera*), with its slender beak, selects the more delicate larch cones.

The crossbill's beak is a multipurpose tool. The bird uses it to wrench a cone free from a tree and then flies with the cone to a safe branch. There, it traps the cone under one foot, inserts the bill under a cone scale, and opens its beak to raise the scale, so exposing the seed beneath. Its tongue whips out to take the seed. The bird also uses its bill, as a parrot does, to haul itself from branch to branch.

Owls and hawks are chief among the taiga's birds of prey. The Eurasian goshawk (*Accipeter gentilis*) relies mainly on its keen eyesight to locate prey. It flies low to hunt or watches from a high vantage point on a branch. The goshawk hunts medium-size birds up to the size of crows and grouse and small mammals, such as hares and squirrels. It relies on speed and agility, using its short wings and long tail to turn in flight to match the movements of its prey.

The great gray owl (*Strix nebulosa*) of North America and Eurasia watches from a high point in a tree, looking and listening for signs of prey. Its ears are placed at slightly different heights on the head. By turning and tilting its head, it can use its stereo hearing to pinpoint the precise location of its prey by sound alone. This ability is particularly useful in winter, when the bird's main prey—voles—are active beneath a thick cover of snow. The owl hovers above its prey, with its thick, downy feathers cushioning the sounds of its wing-beats. It then partially folds its wings to drop noiselessly to the ground, seizing its prey in its talons. Sometimes it enters the snow headfirst and has to dig out its prey before dispatching it with a quick bite to the back of the neck.

## Small mammals

A rarely observed army of small mammals forages and hunts in taiga's trees and on or below the ground. A variety of rodents are dominant among taiga's herbivorous (plant-eating) small mammals. Like rodents elsewhere, they feature well-developed, chisel-like incisor teeth and jaws specialized for gnawing.

The smallest taiga rodents are the forest voles (family Muridae, subfamily Arvicolinae). As adults, they weigh no more than 1.5 ounces (40 g). In winter, they dig tunnels in the snow that connect to the surface by ventilation shafts that bring fresh air. The snow offers good insulation against the chilly air above.

Voles eat a wide range of food. Like many taiga mammals, they change their diet according to seasonal availability. In winter, the vole diet is largely restricted to buried nuts and in fall, soft fruits. In summer, their nourishment extends to leaves, seeds, mushrooms, lichens, thin bark, and insects.

Voles breed rapidly in mild weather and food-rich conditions. They can produce five litters of four to eight young in a season, with a pair capable of producing more than 100 descendants in a year. Voles need to produce plenty of young. Many young voles die before reaching maturity, with most succumbing to starvation or predators.

Members of the family Sciuridae, the squirrel family—including squirrels, chipmunks, and marmots—are widespread across North American and Eurasian taiga. They eat pine seeds and bury cones, nuts, fruits, and other edibles as a winter food supply. Red squirrels of North America (*Tamiasciurus hudsonicus*) and Eurasia (*Sciurus vulgaris*) use their sharp incisor teeth to gnaw through the scales of spruce cones and pinecones to reach the seeds inside. Being active for most of the year, many red squirrels migrate to follow the cone-ripening season of their food trees. Usually, they settle in one treetop location over winter and sleep part of the time in a home constructed of twigs in

## A pale shadow

Some taiga mammals, most notably the stoat and the snowshoe hare, turn pale in winter. This change in fur color is effective camouflage against a snowy background. It enables the hare to better escape its predators and the stoat to more successfully hunt its prey. Pale fur may also offer better insulation. Pale hairs lack the pigment of dark hairs, and so can be thinner, creating more space between the hairs to trap insulating air.

*A snowshoe hare's* (Lepus americanus) *pale winter coloration provides camouflage against the snowy backdrop.* (Courtesy of Tom Mangelsen/Minden Pictures)

the fork between trunk and branches. From this haven they make occasional forays to raid their food stores.

Hares and rabbits can be confused for rodents, but they actually belong to a different group, the lagomorphs. They differ from rodents in various ways, including having a second set of upper incisor teeth and a more delicate skull structure.

The snowshoe hare of Canada (*Lepus americanus*) gains its name from its broad, well-furred feet, which allow it to hop across the surface of deep snow. The hares are noted for their fur and their population cycles (see "Predator-prey cycles," pages 104–105). They shed their fur twice a year, changing from rusty brown and black to almost pure white fur in fall, and then back to the darker color in spring (see the sidebar on page 81). In summer and fall, the hares feed on grasses and on the leaves and fruits of various other herbaceous plants. In winter, they resort to eating conifer needles and the buds, twigs, and bark of woody plants.

The smallest taiga carnivores (meat-eaters) are members of the shrew (Soricidae) and weasel (Mustelidae) families. Several species of shrew live in a typical taiga forest, each favoring slightly different soil conditions. Species that live in the same habitat feed on prey of different sizes. Large shrews favor earthworms, large beetles, and other prey of similar size, while smaller shrews catch a wide variety of beetles, spiders, centipedes, millipedes, and mites. The Eurasian shrew (*Sorex araneus*), common in broad-leaved woodland as well as taiga forest, weighs a paltry half an ounce (14 g) or less. Yet it is a formidable predator and must consume 80–90 percent of its body weight every 24 hours to sustain its incredibly high metabolic rate. It readily bites to defend itself against attack.

Stoats and weasels are widespread in the Eurasian and North American taiga. They are sleek, agile hunters that rush about the forest floor and enter burrows at breakneck speed. Taiga stoats and weasels favor voles as their prey. They chase voles across the forest floor or in burrows and outrun or corner them.

Stoats and weasels mate during the summer. Males grow to nearly twice the weight of females. Even so, the heaviest males only weigh about half a pound (225 g). Males fertilize eggs internally. The fertilized eggs do not implant in the female's womb until many months later, however, delaying pregnancy. This ensures the young are born the following spring, after the thaw, when food is plentiful.

Much larger than weasels and stoats is the European pine marten (*Martes martes*) and its Asian counterpart, the sable (*Martes zibellina*). Both grow to more than four pounds (about 2 kg) and hunt with catlike movements. The pine marten is an adept tree climber. Both animals are omnivorous, eating fruits as well as hunting small rodents, birds, and insects. Most of these they capture on the ground. People have heavily hunted the sable for its prized glossy, dark fur, and the species is now regarded as endangered.

The North American mink (*Mustela vison*) is widely distributed within and beyond the taiga. It is an opportunistic predator, using its partially webbed feet to hunt in freshwater as well as on land. It feeds on fish and crayfish, as well as small birds and rodents. Around 1900, fur trappers took American mink to stock fur farms in Europe and Russia. Some of the animals escaped and have established wild populations. These pose a threat not only to prey species but also to their rival predators, such as the sable in Russia.

## Large mammals

The beaver is the largest taiga rodent. The North American species (*Castor canadensis*) weighs up to about 65 pounds (30 kg) and grows to about 48 inches (120 cm) long including its paddle-like tail. The closely related Eurasian beaver (*Castor fiber*) is slightly larger.

Beavers live in and around lakes and slow-flowing rivers in extended family groups of four to six animals. They fell trees and build dams, so transforming their local environment out of all proportion to their small size. They bring down trees for food (they consume the bark and shoots) and to provide logs and branches to build their dams and their home, called a lodge. Dam building is crucial to a beaver's ability to create a secure home. By regulating a river's water level, beavers can ensure that the entrances to their lodge remain below the water surface. This makes it difficult for predators such as wolves to gain access.

A mating pair of beavers builds a lodge from branches, mud, and stones that they painstakingly assemble to create a central chamber with several submerged entrances. The lodge incorporates a dry sleeping platform that lies above water level. Close by, beavers store wood underwater, which they consume during the winter when the water surface is frozen and they are unable to break through the ice to forage.

A lodge can be an amazingly large construction. The biggest have been measured at 43 feet (13 m) tall—about the height of a four-story house. Beaver dams, too, can be extensive structures. The largest on record was found in Montana. It consisted of several barriers that together formed a system 2,300 feet (700 m) long.

Not all Eurasian beavers build lodges. In suitable watercourses, they will excavate burrows in the banks rather than constructing lodges of wood.

Beavers are excellent divers and swimmers. They can stay submerged, without breathing, for 20 minutes. They are both demolition as well as construction experts. In a single night, an adult beaver can fell a medium-size poplar tree with a

*A North American beaver (Castor canadensis) towing a tree branch. The beaver will use the branch in building a dam or in constructing its home, called a lodge, or the vegetation will be stored as a winter food source. (Courtesy of Shin Yoshino/ Minden Pictures)*

trunk four to five inches (10–12 cm) thick. With the help of family members, it can cut the branches off the trunk, gnaw the branches and trunk into manageable chunks, and carry them off to use or store. A tree can disappear overnight, with only a tree stump and a scattering of wood chips remaining.

People have hunted beavers for many hundreds of years. Their numbers have been greatly reduced, but beavers are still common locally. Beavers were killed for their dense, waterproof fur, because they damage trees (a family unit can fell more than 100 in a year), and because their dams cause flooding (which can damage many more trees). However, the activities of beavers are simply another part of the cycle of life in the taiga. The lake that forms behind a beaver dam eventually becomes silted. Water plants flourish and animals such as the moose come to graze. The decaying plants create peat, and over many decades the former pond becomes colonized by sedges, grasses, and shrubs, which eventually give way to taiga trees.

Except for North America's wood bison (see the sidebar on page 86), deer are the biggest plant-eaters of the taiga. Moose (called elk in Eurasia) and caribou (reindeer) are the largest deer. Moose (*Alces alces*) remain in taiga year-round, except for occasional forays into tundra. Caribou (*Rangifer tarandus*) spend much of the year in tundra and migrate to the taiga to overwinter (see "Migrations," pages 103–104).

The moose is the world's largest deer. Males reach six feet six inches (2 m) at the shoulder and can weigh 1,100 pounds (500 kg). Moose are usually peaceful animals, preferring to melt into the forest rather than confront predators such as wolves or people. In summer, they often favor lakes, where they graze on water plants and eat waterside shoots of willow, birch, and aspen. By submerging in the lake for hours on end, a moose can avoid the attentions of summer's hordes of bloodsucking insects.

Moose have a voracious appetite. They consume up to 33 pounds (15 kg) of tree bark each day in winter and damage tracts of forest in the process. In summer, they average more than 66 pounds (30 kg) of plant leaves and shoots daily.

A healthy moose is a formidable adversary. A grown male can fend off all but the worst wolf attacks. Its deadly weapons

## Wood bison

Some biologists recognize the wood bison as a subspecies of the American bison (*Bison bison*) and distinct from the plains bison that lives to the south. Certain recent genetic evidence supports this view. However, some of Canada's wood bison have interbred with plains bison in the last few decades, so the numbers of the pure subspecies is quite limited.

Wood bison (*Bison bison athabascae*) are slightly larger than the plains subspecies (*Bison bison bison*), with males reaching about 10 feet (3 m) at the shoulder and weighing more than one U.S. ton (910 kg). Wood bison graze on grasses and sedges in natural meadows amid the taiga forest. These include areas that flood regularly close to rivers and lakes and elsewhere where fires regularly clear the forest. In the fall, the bison enter the forest to feed on lichen.

Like the plains bison, the wood bison nearly became extinct due to overhunting by European settlers in the 19th century. This clearance helped pave the way for settlers to ranch cattle and grow crops. It was also probably part of a strategy to clear the land of native peoples who hunted the bison. Various estimates suggest the wood-bison population fell from more than 150,000 animals in the early 1800s to about 300 in the 1890s. Attempts to save the subspecies raised their numbers to more than 1,500 by 1922, when the Wood Buffalo National Park (WBNP) was set up in Alberta. These bison interbred with plains bison to produce hybrids. They also contracted the cattle diseases brucellosis and tuberculosis, which weaken them and make them more vulnerable to predation and the cold during winter months. However, in 1957, wildlife officials discovered a pure, disease-free wood bison herd in part of the WBNP, and 18 of these animals formed the basis for a herd that now numbers about 2,000. Current conservation efforts are aimed at keeping the pure, disease-free herds separate from hybrid or diseased stock.

are unusually sharp hooves and massive antlers up to 79 inches (2 m) across. More often, however, males use their antlers as weapons in ritual fights with other males over access to females.

Taiga's large predators range widely to find sufficient prey, and they are opportunists, turning to carrion if fresh meat is not available. The lynx needs an average of two to four pounds (1–2 kg) of meat a day and gets it by hunting a variety of animals, from voles to small deer. In winter, the main diet of the North American lynx (*Lynx canadensis*) is the snowshoe hare.

Winter is a time of hardship for the lynx, and in years with poor hunting, some lynx starve. The high-speed chase to catch a snowshoe hare in snow can cover 650 feet (200 m) and consumes a considerable amount of energy. A lynx cannot afford too many misses. Lack of food can dull its energy and reduce the chances of successful hunting.

Large predators struggle to hunt in the deep snow of the taiga in winter. The exception is the wolverine (*Gulo gulo*), called the glutton in Eurasia. This giant member of the weasel family grows to about 60 pounds (27 kg) and has broad feet that act like snowshoes. Its fur is dense and long and does not retain ice or snow.

For most of its life the wolverine is a solitary animal, coming together with other adults only to mate or at times of food shortage, when more than one wolverine may scavenge a large carcass. Females give birth to two or three cubs from mid- to late winter. The female feeds and protects her young in a den under snow. By the end of the first summer, the young are able to fend for themselves and leave the protection of their mother.

*A male moose (Alces alces) chewing vegetation grazed from the bottom of a taiga lake. The moose, called "elk" in Eurasia, is the world's largest deer.* (Courtesy of Tim Fitzharris/ Minden Pictures)

*A pack of gray wolves (Canis lupus) at a deer kill in Minnesota. By hunting cooperatively, wolves can capture animals much larger than themselves. (Courtesy of Jim Brandenberg/ Minden Pictures)*

Wolverines have strength and aggression out of proportion to their size. In winter, a single wolverine can take on and kill an adult moose or caribou struggling in deep snow. They also eat carrion, and some wolverines follow wolf packs to finish off uneaten scraps. Hungry wolverines have even been known to drive bears away from their kill. In the abundance of summer and fall, wolverines have an omnivorous diet of small rodents, bird eggs and hatchlings, insects, wild fruit, and pine seeds.

Few people have seen a wolverine in the wild. With their cautious, secretive nature and their adept hunting skills, wolverines regularly steal the bait from traps set for other fur-bearing animals. They are rarely caught themselves.

Gray wolves (*Canis lupus*), found throughout the taiga range, from Alaska eastward to Far East Asia, are the only large taiga predators that hunt cooperatively. Typically, they live in a pack of eight to 12 wolves led by a dominant pair. In summer, when food is plentiful, the pack often splits into smaller groups or individuals that hunt fairly small prey, such as voles and hares. In winter, prey are more scarce, and the wolves tend to stay in a pack and hunt larger animals such as caribou (reindeer) and moose (elk) that may be up to 10 times a wolf's weight.

Wolves usually find and track their prey by smell, often at distances of more than one mile (1.6 km). Once a quarry is located, the pack huddles together—exchanging messages through movement, posture, and growls—before setting off in pursuit. When wolves approach a prey animal, it is the flight of the victim that triggers the final attack. The wolves take turns jumping onto the victim and biting it. Gradually the animal is weakened by injury, shock, and blood loss and is overpowered. The pack tears the prey to pieces, with each animal gulping down as much as 20 pounds (9 kg) of meat at a sitting.

Despite the wolves' savage pack hunting, they are generally quite timid creatures and have little direct contact with humans. Claims of wolves attacking and killing people are rarely substantiated, whereas humans have been responsible for decimating many wolf populations in the last 200 years.

The brown bear (*Ursus arctos*) is by far the largest predator of the taiga, although its diet is largely plant matter, and it rarely kills anything larger than a salmon. Many biologists recognize at least three subspecies of brown bear—the grizzly and Kodiak subspecies and a smaller Eurasian subspecies.

## Salmon feast

Prior to their winter sleep, brown bears in coastal regions of Alaska, Canada, and Russia feast on salmon that are making their way upriver to spawn. The fish gather in pools at the base of rapids and waterfalls before fighting their way upstream. Bears gather to grab fish with their jaws or pounce on them with their paws. The salmon's flesh, rich in oil and protein, helps sustain the bears during their long winter sleep.

The largest male brown bears (females are smaller in stature) reach more than nine feet (2.8 m) at the shoulder and weigh as much as one U.S. ton (910 kg). A brown bear has extremely powerful forelimbs, with sharp claws to dig for edible roots and bulbs. A bear will take berries, fungi, insects, small mammals, and carrion, depending on availability, which varies with the season. Most bears are solitary and shy away from human contact unless attracted to camp sites by food supplies or edible trash that have been left unsecured. With its bulky body and powerful paws, a bear makes a formidable adversary. A brown bear can kill and eat a moose (elk) if the opportunity presents itself.

# CHAPTER 5

# TAIGA ECOLOGY

When biologists study the environment (the living and non-living surroundings), they often choose an area with recognizable boundaries and analyze biological relationships and processes within that locality. They define this area as an *ecosystem*. It consists of a community of organisms (microbes, larger fungi, plants, and animals) together with the *habitat* or locality in which they live. Ecologists are biologists who study the populations of organisms within an ecosystem.

In the taiga forest, the forest canopy, the leaf litter, and a sphagnum bog are all examples of ecosystems. The taiga forest as a whole is an ecosystem and, on a much smaller scale, so is a rotting fallen tree. Ecologists decide the size of the ecosystem based on the processes and interactions they wish to study.

An ecosystem must be definable, but its edges may not be distinct. The dense taiga forest, for example, rarely comes to an abrupt halt at its borders—except where people have altered the environment, as by felling the edges of the forest and creating fields alongside. Usually taiga grades gradually into the ecosystems that surround it. On its northern border, taiga trees gradually thin out and become scattered, giving way to tundra. On its southern border, conifer forest gives way to mixed conifer and broad-leaved forest or to grasslands. Among scientists, there is a difference in opinion as to the exact boundaries of the taiga biome, which means that estimates of the area of the world's taiga vary from one expert authority to another.

## Energy flow, food chains, and food webs

Sunlight provides the energy that sustains the forest ecosystem. Sunlight energy is trapped by plants and is passed on to animals as chemical energy when animals consume plants (or later, when animals consume other animals). Useful chemical components that organisms need to build their bodies originate from the underlying bedrock and are made available by weathering, the breakdown of rock by physical, chemical, and biological processes. Once these chemicals are absorbed by plants or microbes, they tend to be recycled by the community of organisms within the ecosystem. Energy flows through the community of organisms in an ecosystem and is ultimately lost to the environment as heat energy. Nutrients, however, are recycled.

To understand how ecosystems function, ecologists usually start by examining feeding relationships: Who eats what? They gather this information in many ways, such as observing feeding behavior, studying the gut contents of animals, or using radioactive tracers to track substances as they pass from one organism to another. At its simplest, this information is summarized in a *food chain,* a flow diagram with arrows pointing from the organism that is eaten to the organisms that eats it. Plants are often the first step, or link, in the chain because they make their own food and other creatures depend upon plants—directly or indirectly—for their food supplies. Because plants manufacture food, ecologists call them *producers.* In taiga, conifer trees are the main producers.

Each link or level in a food chain is called a trophic (feeding) level, and most plants are at the first level. Plant-eating animals form the second link in a food chain. Ecologists call them *primary consumers.* In taiga, a wide variety of animals feed upon conifer trees. Seed-eating birds, such as crossbills and nuthatches, and rodents such as squirrels consume the cones themselves, the seeds within them, or both. Various insects, their larvae, and some birds eat conifer needles. Deer eat tree bark, and many types of insect and fungi consume tree wood. Deer, voles, and various birds are among those that dine on the shoots and leaves of herbaceous plants and the fruits of forest shrubs.

Larger animals, classified as *secondary consumers,* eat primary consumers. In boreal forests they include woodpeckers, which eat bark-eating beetles; spiders and centipedes that eat woodlice (pill bugs); and lynxes, which eat hares.

At the fourth trophic level, larger predators (*tertiary consumers*) eat secondary consumers. Birds of prey, for example, such as the goshawk, eat insect-eating birds, and wolves, given the opportunity, will consume smaller predatory animals such as shrews.

Without organisms to break down and recycle dead matter on the forest floor, the ground would soon become covered in a thick layer of leaf litter and fallen branches and tree trunks. Decomposers accelerate the breakdown of dead microbes, plants, and animals, and they recycle the chemical locked up in these organisms so they are returned to the soil. Much of the leaf litter on the taiga forest floor takes five years or more to break down completely, but without decomposers, this process would take longer. Despite their importance, decomposers are often omitted from food chains.

Food chains are great simplifications of the real situation in nature. When drawing a food chain, an ecologist often uses a single species to represent dozens at each trophic level. At higher trophic levels, many species consume organisms from more than one of the lower trophic levels. So, for example, a goshawk eats both seed- and insect-eating birds and is both a secondary and a tertiary consumer. Many taiga mammals, ranging from voles to bears, are omnivores (they eat both plant and animal matter). They are primary consumers but are secondary and even tertiary consumers as well.

To show feeding relationships more realistically, biologists draw complex flow charts called *food webs* that incorporate many food chains. Even these are a simplification. They show only a few dozen of the hundreds of species involved, and they typically omit symbiotic relationships (see the sidebar "Types of symbiosis," page 95). Likewise, it is difficult to incorporate the dynamics of a living ecosystem, with diets changing with season of the year and age of the animal, and with animals migrating in and out of the region.

The number of trophic levels in a food chain is rarely more than five. Only a small proportion of the energy at one trophic level is passed on to the next. Trees, for example, use up much of their food supply in respiration (the process of releasing energy to power metabolic functions that keep the organism alive). And not all the components of a tree—such

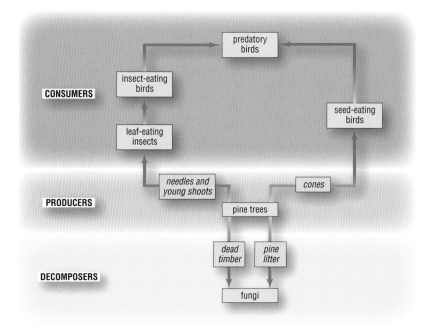

*Part of a generalized food web for a conifer forest*

as the tough substance called lignin that gives wood much of its strength—are readily digestible. Respiration and indigestibility operate at other trophic levels as well, with the result that only about 10 percent of the energy in one trophic level is passed on to the next. This limits the number of trophic levels that an ecosystem can sustain.

To visualize the flow of energy through an ecosystem, ecologists today often resort to drawing an *energy pyramid*. Gathering the data to construct such a pyramid is time consuming and labor intensive but yields extremely useful information. Scientists use light meters to measure the amount of sunlight that plants are exposed to over the year. They take tissue samples from local plants and animals, dry them out, and burn them in sensitive devices called calorimeters that measure the amount of energy released. This gives the scientists values for the amount of chemical energy stored temporarily at different trophic levels. They note how the populations of plants and animals grow and decline with season and from year to year. They analyze the stomach contents of animals, and they trace how much dead material trees shed each year, how much waste matter animals produce, and how decom-

## Types of symbiosis

*Parasitism, commensalism,* and *mutualism* are types of close association between different species that fall under the umbrella term *symbiosis.*

Parasites are organisms that live in or on other organisms, their hosts, at the expense of the host. For example, many mammals harbor flatworm parasites called tapeworms that live in the gut. The tapeworms absorb nutrients, depriving their host of some food, and their presence can irritate and inflame the gut. However, tapeworms rarely cause sufficient damage to kill the host. For simplicity, scientists often omit parasites from food chains and food webs. However, most larger organisms are host to at least one type of animal parasite; a conifer tree typically harbors dozens.

Mutualism is a relationship where both partners benefit, such as in mycorrhizae—the association between fungi and trees (see "Partners beneath the soil," pages 68–69). In commensalism, the commensal organism benefits but the host is neither harmed nor benefited, a result that is difficult for scientists to demonstrate one way or the other. Other birds that follow closely in the wake of a woodpecker to consume any insects the woodpecker has disturbed could loosely be regarded as commensals.

posers process the dead or waste matter. In this way, scientists gradually piece together the patterns of energy flow through the ecosystem.

Such detailed analyses provide biologists with the data they need to manage ecosystems and to work out the impacts of environmental changes, both natural and human-induced. They can see the effect of grazers and parasites on the growth of trees. They can also work out whether a forest is growing (increasing its biomass) year on year, remaining roughly stable, or declining. Such information is clearly of great interest to foresters (see the last chapter).

## Renewal and succession

The leaf litter of the forest floor—most of it conifer needles with a hard, waxy coating—breaks down relatively slowly. Months of rainfall wash the toxins out of the needles. As the needles weather, they become brittle, and small animals can consume and digest them more easily. The army of needle-eating animals includes earthworms, springtail insects, soil mites, and wood lice (pill bugs). The plant remains pass through the guts of these animals—often through one animal after another. Soil fungi and bacteria complete the decay process, releasing the plant nutrients back into the soil.

The community that inhabits an ecosystem is built up over time, and, as we have seen in the long term, the species composition of a community changes in response to climatic and other environmental shifts (see "Taiga advance and retreat," pages 53–55). The way a community develops in a given climate with a particular set of soil conditions often follows a more or less predictable pattern. This pattern—where some species in a community are replaced by others in an orderly sequence—is called an *ecological succession.*

Imagine the situation where a moving glacier has scraped off all the topsoil covering a rocky outcrop and then receded, leaving behind the bare rock. Microbes and visible algae and lichens are the first organisms to colonize the rock. They form the *pioneer community* that grows without an established soil. Within a few years, the rock weathers, and the community of organisms leaves debris that contributes to a developing soil layer. Now larger plant species, such as mosses and ferns, can invade. In time, the soil will be sufficiently developed and rich in nutrients to enable seed-bearing plants such as grasses, herbs, shrubs, and eventually trees to establish themselves. Together with the plants lives an accompanying community of animals. The community that ultimately develops—in many cool temperate environments, a plant community dominated by trees—is called the *climax community.*

The type of succession just described is called a *primary succession* because bare rock is the starting point; it is, as it were, a clean slate. In reality, such successions rarely occur today in the taiga biome (although they do happen in regions of volcanic activity, where new rock is laid down). However, primary successions have happened many times in Earth's recent geological history in thaws that follow glacial periods. Secondary successions—where most of the vegetation is removed, but the starting point is other than bare rock—are much more common in the taiga. They occur, for example, when loggers clear an area of trees but do not plant replacements or when a natural fire clears part of the forest.

Ecologists sometimes call the entire sequence in an ecological succession a *sere*. The different stages in the sequence are called *seral stages*. The American grassland ecologist Frederic E. Clements (1874–1945) first described the concept in detail in the 1910s based on his observations of North American land vegetation. According to Clements, for a given climate there is a climax community that ultimately develops. Even if landscape features, microclimate, land use, or other factors prevent the establishment of the climax community, given enough time, the climatic climax community will eventually develop. In temperate climates, the climax community on land is a woodland, whether coniferous, broad-leaved, or a mixture of the two.

Ecologists, while recognizing Clements's great contribution in developing the concept of succession, now regard his idea of a climatic climax community as rather too simplistic. In many cases, factors such as fire, soil type, or human interference (such as grazing animals maintaining grassland) prevent the notional climax from ever developing. Today's ecologists favor the concept of a *polyclimax,* in which a region supports a number of potential climaxes. In parts of southwest Canada, recurrent fires will maintain a "climax" community of pine rather than spruce. Very damp soil conditions throughout the year are likely to favor black spruce over white.

Knowing the likely form of a succession in a given environment, land-use planners can manage the succession. Planting conifer trees of the right kind could accelerate the succession, or cropping certain kinds of tree could arrest it.

## Fire in the taiga

In taiga regions with a continental climate (fairly dry year-round, cold in winter, and warm in summer), the ground cover is often crisp and dry in late spring and early summer. These are favorable conditions for ground fires. Lightning strikes, or sparks or flames set by people, can easily light the dry tinder on the ground and start a fire. Conifer trees often retain dead needles for long periods, and these burn readily, causing crown fires that advance rapidly from tree to tree. Ground or crown fires will kill trees if the cambium, the cylinder of actively growing tissue in the tree trunk, is subjected to temperatures above approximately 150°F (65°C).

## Fire shapes the taiga

When fires reach the tree canopy and burn away branches under intense heat, all tree species suffer, and many of the affected trees will die. With the ground clear of vegetation and light now able to reach the forest floor, the conditions are in place for a secondary succession. Initially, broad-leaved trees replace the conifers, beginning with birches and aspens. They are as cold-resistant as many conifers but need more light. They are given the opportunity to thrive when fire—or some other factor—creates a clearing in the forest. In bright sunlight, the aspens and birches grow faster than conifers and reach their full height within 40 or 50 years. Meanwhile, conifers grow in their shade. In time, the conifers grow through the broad-leaved canopy and begin to overshadow the birches, aspens, and poplars. Gradually, the conifers replace the broad-leaved trees because close to the ground there is low light intensity that favors young conifers over young broad-leaved trees. At the same time, the light-demanding shrubs and herbaceous plants that thrived in the early stages of the succession begin to disappear and become replaced by the shade-tolerant species typical of the taiga.

There is a succession among the conifers too. If conditions are not too wet or too dry, then the firs and spruces of the dark taiga will eventually replace the larches and pines of the light taiga. However, the succession to dark taiga is halted if ground fires are common. In this case, larches and pines remain as the climax vegetation.

(opposite page)
*Succession after a forest fire*

Although fires can be catastrophic for plants and animals in the short term, in the long life of a forest, natural fires are opportunities for renewal (see sidebar). In light taiga forest, larches and most pines have thick bark and deep roots and shrug off ground fires fairly well. The jack pine, in fact, depends upon fire to burst its cones open and release their

old-growth forest before a severe forest fire

early stage in succession after a fire, broad-leaved trees dominate

late stage in succession, conifer trees dominate

seeds. In dark taiga, on the other hand, the resident spruces and firs have shallower roots and thinner bark. Many die after only weak ground fires. This is one reason why the larches of light taiga tend to dominate regions with very continental climates, such as eastern Siberia. Here fairly frequent summer fires are coupled with winter temperatures that are bitterly cold.

Fire, by opening up the canopy and offering opportunities for young trees to grow, can increase the biological diversity of the forest. Fire helps kill outbreaks of tree pests and diseases, and the ashes release nutrients back into the soil, encouraging renewed plant growth. However, scientists and environmentalists are concerned that fires set by people— usually to clear land for agriculture or industry, or to manage a landscape for hunting or mushroom picking—may overwhelm the ability of a forest to regenerate. Repeated ground fires that smolder at high temperatures for long periods alter the structure and composition of the soil. They burn away humus and make the soil much more likely to be eroded and washed away (see "Fires," pages 149–150).

## Animals surviving winter

Although most taiga birds migrate south out of the taiga in winter, there are some notable exceptions. Crossbills breed in the taiga winter. They build nests of twigs in the branches of trees. Even in these snug nests lined with fine vegetable matter, temperatures can fall as low as –31°F (–35°C) for short periods. The adults forage for seeds inside cones, which they bring back to feed their chicks. In winter, pine trees are festooned with cones, and crossbills are among the few birds that can pry them open for their seeds. For them, the winter is the time of greatest food supply, which is why they breed at this time despite the cold.

Nutcrackers overwinter in the taiga but do not breed there, probably because the seeds they favor belong to trees that shed their cones in the fall. Nutcrackers suffer a food shortage in winter. In fall, they store caches of cones under fallen branches, next to stumps, or in the ground, which they raid during the winter.

The capercaillies of Eurasia—giants among taiga birds—spend wintry days in the branches of trees, where they consume pine needles. At dusk, they return to ground level and bury themselves in snow to spend the night. The spruce grouse of North America, like the capercaillie of Eurasia, overwinters in the taiga, feeding mostly on pine needles. It, too, has a specialized digestive system that enables it to gain the maximum amount of energy from low-calorie conifer needles.

Among the smaller birds that overwinter in the Eurasian taiga, woodpeckers, nuthatches, and willow tits form mixed flocks. It seems likely that the other birds benefit from the insects and seeds that the woodpeckers expose after they have finished exploring tree trunks and cones for food.

Animals other than birds generally adopt one of two strategies to survive the grim winters. Some migrate to slightly warmer climates—usually to the south—where food remains available. Others reduce their activity to a minimum and survive with the help of stored food supplies in their environment or fat supplies stored within the body.

In winter, most insects seek havens beneath tree bark, underground, or even underwater. Overwintering as an egg or a larva is one way of surviving the bitter winter months with minimal energy expenditure. Caterpillars of the black-veined white butterfly, for example, survive in a cradle of hawthorn leaves that they bind around themselves with woven silk. Some insects produce natural antifreeze in their body fluids to combat freezing.

Red squirrels—along with some seed-eating taiga birds such as jays and nutcrackers—are hoarders. They bury food in the forest floor and hope to return to it during the winter. (Squirrels' forgotten hoards are one form of seed dispersal.) Squirrels hoard a much wider variety of food items than most other taiga animals. Although they favor cones, they will also stash nuts and mushrooms underground or in holes in tree trunks. One squirrel can stash away 200 cones in a single day.

Most species of squirrel sleep for days at a time during the winter, waking for short periods to feast on food stores before returning to sleep. But some types of squirrel, such as marmots and chipmunks, are true hibernators. They hide away in burrows or hollow tree trunks and become immobile and seemingly lifeless. In fact, their body functions continue but, in many cases, at a fraction of the normal rate. Body temperature falls from its normal of nearly 104°F (40°C) to less than 50°F (10°C). Breathing rate and heartbeat drop to well below normal.

Marmots, burrow-dwelling members of the squirrel family found in North America and Eurasia, hibernate for up to eight months of the year. They do not feed at all during this time. They wake every two to three weeks to dispose of urine, and they rouse themselves during the harshest days of winter, when there is a danger of freezing to death.

The eastern chipmunk of North America and the Siberian chipmunk, by contrast, interrupt their hibernation with longer breaks. They store seeds in underground chambers close to the nest. Every few weeks they wake and raid the larder before returning to their slumbers.

Brown bears, contrary to popular belief, are not true hibernators. Their large size helps make hibernation unnecessary (see the sidebar "Size matters"). In winter, they retreat to a den dug in the ground, a natural cave, or a thicket of vegetation. For much of the winter they lie dormant in a sleeping state in which body functions drop only slightly below normal. Body temperature, for example, typically drops from about 100°F (38°C) to 95°F (35°C). Bears

## Size matters

In cool environments, being large can be an advantage. Animals lose body heat across the body surface. Size for size, a large animal has a smaller area of body surface compared to its volume or mass than a smaller animal. So there is a heat-saving premium in being large. Male stoats from northern Canada average about three times the weight of stoats in mild-climate U.S. states. The heat-conserving advantage of a large size also helps explain why the taiga's capercaillie is the world's biggest grouse, the wolverine the largest weasel, and the moose, or elk, the bulkiest deer.

are readily able to rouse themselves if disturbed. Females give birth during the winter and wake regularly to suckle their vulnerable, hairless young, which lie snug in the den with their mother. From spring to fall, adult bears eat vast amounts of food to lay down fat reserves to sustain them over the winter. It is common for a bear to lose more than one-fifth of its body weight during winter, as it uses up its fat reserves. A skinny version of its former self emerges from the den in spring.

Many birds leave the taiga in autumn, flying south to warmer climes, where food is available, and then returning the following spring to nest.

## Migrations

Spring in the taiga is filled with the sound of birdsong. Many of the new arrivals are passerines (birds with feet adapted for perching on branches). The birds have overwintered hundreds or thousands of miles to the south. Now they have returned to feed on taiga insects and to establish their nests, sometimes in the very same trees in which they nested the previous year. The tree, ground, and flying insects are abundant enough to provide food for the adult birds and their nestlings.

The number of birds that arrive each spring depends on the success of the migrators in their southern overwintering grounds. At times of adverse weather conditions, their food supplies may fail. Too many birds may compete for too little food, and many of the birds starve to death or may succumb to the cold.

Taiga mammals also migrate with the changing seasons to find food and avoid the worst of the wintry weather. In the fall, caribou in North America and wild reindeer in Eurasia migrate from the tundra to the northern taiga forests to avoid deep snow and search for food. They favor wet clearings in the forest, where they can find lichens, such as reindeer moss, beneath the snow. In North America, a migrating herd may number in the hundreds and may trek more than 620 miles (1,000 km) between tundra and taiga, swimming across rivers and sea inlets on the way. On the return leg in spring, pregnant females take the lead.

The red squirrel of North America, and its relative in Eurasia, regularly migrates to find fresh cones on which to feed. The squirrels travel long distances at more than two mph (3 km/h). Eurasian squirrels will even swim across wide rivers such as Siberia's Yenisey, which is often one mile (1.6 km) wide, to reach new feeding grounds.

## Predator-prey cycles

In the harsh climate of the taiga, many of the small-to-medium-size mammals experience dramatic changes in population size from one year to the next. Often these changes show a pattern that repeats itself every few years. Scientists first revealed this pattern by analyzing the financial accounts of the Hudson Bay Company, which go back to about 1800. The number of fur pelts delivered by trappers each year is a good indication of the abundance of that animal.

The snowshoe hare and its major predator, the lynx, appear to be locked in a population cycle that repeats itself every eight to 11 years. The snowshoe hare population gradually builds year on year and then peaks. At its height the hare population can be 100 times larger than when the population hits a trough. The peak in the lynx population tends to lag one or two years behind the hare population.

Biologists often describe the hare-lynx population cycle as a classic predator-prey cycle, with the number of predators limited by the abundance of their prey. It is often assumed that the lynx control the hare numbers and contribute to the peaks and troughs of the hare population. However, similar fluctuations in hare populations occur even in regions where lynxes are absent. The hare population seems to crash, in part, because they consume the available food and afterward many starve. In winter, the food supply is lean, and the young shoots on which the hares feed lie buried beneath the snow. In years when the hare population peaks, trappers and hunters often find hares that have starved to death. Stress and disease may be other factors that cause hare numbers to crash.

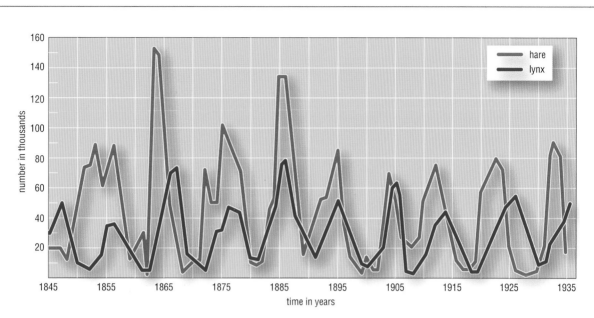

Populations of birds of prey also fluctuate based on the supply of their main prey animals. Voles have population cycles that repeat themselves every three or four years. The vole-hunting great gray owl is widely distributed in the boreal forests of North America, Europe, and Asia. In years when voles are scarce, the owls do not attempt to breed.

*Variation in the abundance of lynx* (Lynx canadensis) *and snowshoe hare* (Lepus americanus) *based on records of the Hudson Bay Company*

# CHAPTER 6

# THE TAIGA IN HISTORY AND PREHISTORY

In a book that emphasizes science, why study history and culture? There are several good reasons. First, a biome such as the taiga is not a static system that remains essentially unchanged millennium after millennium. As explained in chapter 3, the location and composition of the taiga forest has shifted considerably in the last 11,000 years. Changing climate has played a major role but so, both directly and indirectly, have people. For several thousand years, native taiga peoples have been custodians of the taiga we inherit today. Knowing how traditional peoples have exploited the taiga helps us to understand how the biome today has taken its present form, with its particular assemblages of plants and animals.

Second, many traditional taiga peoples, if not exactly living in harmony with taiga environments, appear not to have ruthlessly exploited them to the same extent that industrial societies have. Traditional peoples provide insight as to how the taiga might be exploited in a sustainable way, making use of its full range of resources.

Third, values are important. How the taiga could or should be managed is not based on purely scientific principles. Many factors—environmental, social, and economic—affect decisions about how the taiga might be exploited sustainably. In any case, to think that scientists are completely objective in their work is wrongheaded. What scientists value affects their work. Why are far more people interested in studying songbirds that researching fungi? Fungi, in their role as decomposers, parasites, and as mycorrhizal partners of trees, are arguably more important components of taiga communities than birds. But this is not reflected in the level of human interest. Studying traditional taiga communities helps reveal what it is about the boreal forest that there is to value. And this forms part of our understanding as to why and how we should manage taiga communities, a topic that will be addressed further in the last chapter.

Taiga environments have been inhabited by people for tens of thousands of years, but they have never harbored a vast population. Most of the taiga biome is too cold, with too short a growing season and relatively poor soils, to favor clearance of the land for agriculture or grazing. The peoples in more than two-thirds of the taiga have traditionally made their living from hunting, fishing, trapping, and gathering wild plant products. Such an economy can support only a fairly small population. In the northern and middle taiga regions, this averages out to more than four square miles (10 km²) of land supporting only one person.

The colonization of dense taiga has always been challenging because of the harsh climate and because the dense covering of trees and extensive bogs make travel slow and arduous. Early peoples entered the taiga most easily along major rivers, such as the Lena, Ob, and Yenisey in Russia, and North America's Mackenzie and Yukon. These rivers (some are among the largest in the world) flow roughly south to north and have extensive networks of tributaries. They remain key transport networks.

Despite the challenging nature of much of the taiga landscape and climate, a great deal of the southern taiga, with its milder climate and easier access, has been radically altered within the last 2,000 years. Many generations of people in southern Scandinavia and the central part of European Russia have cleared parts of the taiga forest to grow hardy food crops and raise cattle on a relatively small scale. In such places, the human population density has reached 130 people per square mile (about 50 people/km²).

The last century has seen towns and cities spring up in the Canadian and Russian taiga, often close to where mineral deposits have been discovered. These industrialized townships are in striking contrast to the small, dispersed, traditional taiga communities.

## Origins of taiga peoples

Evidence gathered by climatologists about past climates, when combined with archaeological data about prehistoric

# The Bering land bridge (Beringia)

The Old World (Eurasia and Africa) and the New World (the Americas) meet at the Bering Strait, which today is about 55 miles (89 km) across. On several occasions lasting thousands of years between about 40,000 and 13,000 years ago, sea levels were much lower than today. Ice was locked on land in valley glaciers and ice sheets, and less water than before flowed back into the sea. At such times, the Bering Strait was not covered in seawater but

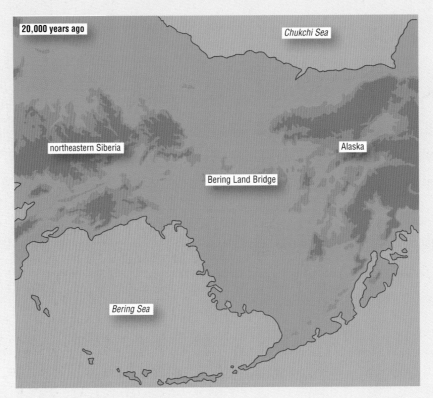

*The Bering land bridge 20,000 years ago*

people and that compiled by human geneticists (those who study the inherited characteristics of humans), point to all of today's peoples descending from those living in Africa some 150,000 years ago. Since then, their descendants have migrated to different parts of the globe and evolved to become the different racial groups we know today.

was dry land forming the Bering land bridge (or Beringia). At times the bridge was hundreds of miles wide from north to south.

The sea level was at its lowest, and the Bering land bridge at its largest, some 18,000–20,000 years ago. People could have walked across from Asia to North America at that time or on other occasions before or since. Descendants of these early American colonizers could also have walked the return journey, from North America to Asia. At times when the Bering land bridge was intact, or even when partly drowned, people could have migrated between the two continents in small sea craft, traveling along coastlines or skirting south of pack ice.

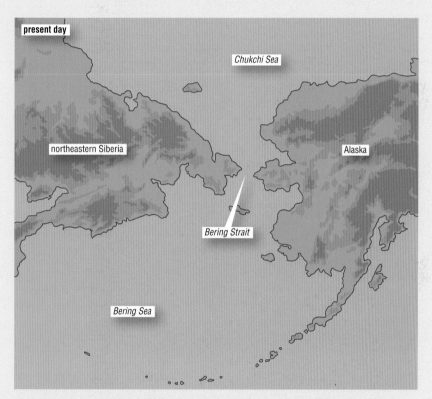

*The Bering land bridge now lies under the waters of the Bering Strait.*

With a major glacial period beginning some 70,000 years ago, glaciers pushed plants, animals, and humans southward. At that time, just south of the ice sheets lay the dry, cold, treeless expanses of the steppe-tundra. By some 45,000 to 35,000 years ago, people that later were to inhabit the taiga were living in southern Europe and hunting on the steppe-tundra. They had a varied diet, which included plant produce gathered from the countryside and meat from animals they hunted. In particular, the people of this period are noted for hunting large plant-eating mammals, including the mammoth, woolly rhinoceros, bison, taiga antelope, and horse. These animals are the so-called *megafauna* (from the Greek *megas,* meaning "great," and *fauna,* a Latin word referring to animals).

Some of these megafauna hunters spread northward into steppe-tundra at latitudes where taiga exists today. At that time (the Siberian Old Stone Age or Paleolithic, spanning the period 40,000–20,000 B.C.E.), some of these people lived in caves. Others lived in dwellings with walls of mammoth bones and roofs supported by reindeer antlers and covered with animal skins. The hunters and their families wore jewelry and ritually buried their dead. Reliable evidence for people settling in the Eurasian taiga region dates to about 25,000 B.C.E. in the Lake Baikal region and at a similar time along the major river systems of the Ob, Yenisey, and Lena.

At the start of the Middle Stone Age (about 20,000 B.C.E. in Siberia), Siberian peoples began to use more sophisticated stone implements. They mastered the ability to shape flints into thin, keen-edged blades, called microliths or microblades. These could be as sharp as a razor, and inserted into a wood or bone handle, they formed a knife or arrow with a replaceable blade.

By 13,000 B.C.E., the retreat of glaciers and ice sheets was substantial, and Eurasian peoples had settled widely across Siberia and the Far East. By this time, some Eurasian people had migrated across a land bridge to colonize North America (see the sidebar on pages 108–109). Such colonization may already have occurred many thousands of years earlier.

By 11,000 B.C.E., Siberia's climate was warming. Extensive boreal forests began to establish themselves, replacing the tundra steppes. The steppe-dwelling large herbivores began to decline. Hunters now turned to elk as their main prey.

## The first Americans

The earliest well-documented evidence of human occupation of the Americas by a recognizable culture dates to about 9,000–9,500 B.C.E. These are the so-called Clovis people, named after the site in Clovis, New Mexico, where their implements were first found. The Clovis made flaked tools with features for attaching flints to shafts. These early settlers used the atlatl, or spear thrower, which acted as an extension of the throwing arm to propel a spear with great force. Such people could have hunted the big game of the North American plains. Many archaeologists suspect that their hunting contributed to the extinction of much of the big game of North America, including the elephant-like mammoths and mastodons, ground sloths, and camels. Many climatologists favor climate change as the main factor responsible for the extinction of these animals at around this time.

In 1986, a landmark paper published in *Current Anthropology* by Joseph Greenberg, Christy Turner, and Stephen Zegura reviewed the evidence for the early colonization of the Americas. They concluded that at least three migrations from Eurasia were involved, and the first (Clovis people) must have happened at least 12,000 years ago, with Athabascan peoples (today found in Alaska and in northwestern and central Canada) arriving several thousand years later. Greenberg, Turner, and Zegura's work was based on bringing together the evidence from comparing the genetics, teeth structure, and languages of present-day native peoples in the Americas and Asia. The more similar the features in different peoples, the closer they are likely to be related. The work done by other researchers since has complicated the picture, with different methods yielding results that are not always in agreement.

Modern techniques of recombinant DNA technology enable researchers to analyze genetic material directly. This reveals genetic similarities and differences between existing human populations and suggests which populations are most closely related and how recently they might have separated. Unfortunately, such investigations have given rise to a number of different possible explanations, with anywhere from one to six migrations accounting for the distributions of American peoples observed today. Some of these studies push back the time scale for the colonization of North America to more than 20,000 years ago.

When people first colonized the Americas may never be known. Almost certainly the first settlers moved along coastlines and riverbanks. Fish and other aquatic mammals are rich sources of protein, fat, and vitamins particularly important for people in cold, inhospitable climates. Early settlement sites close to the sea and rivers would have been inundated by rising water levels as the climate warmed. There is hope, however, that clues to the earliest occupation of the Americas might one day be revealed by underwater archaeologists diving in shallow waters.

In North America, boreal forests recolonized the southern Yukon by about 8000 B.C.E. Hunters followed and moved into the Great Slave and Great Bear Lakes areas of northwest Canada. By 6000 B.C.E., Lake Agassiz, a giant glacial lake that once extended across the plains of the northern United States and into Canada west of the Great Lakes region, was shrinking to a fraction of its former size. People began settling in Ontario, Manitoba, and Saskatchewan.

Within the last 5,000 years, the North American taiga took on much of its present character and became occupied by scattered bands of seminomadic people. To the east lived Algonquian speakers, such as the ancestors of today's native speakers of Cree, Montagnais-Naskapi, Ojibwa, or Saulteaux. To the northwest lay various Athabascan-speaking tribes, including the Tanaina, Tana, Han, and Hara, who live west of the Great Bear and Great Slave Lakes, and Yellowknife and other Chippewa, who live to the east.

The Algonquians and Athabascans both developed lifestyles that combined fishing in rivers and lakes with hunting large plant-eating mammals such as caribou and moose. They also incorporated a gatherer lifestyle, making use of wild fruits and roots for foods and medicines (see the sidebar "Taiga medicine," page 119). Outside North America's taiga zone, along the Pacific coast, Inuit (Eskimo) and Athabascan peoples adopted lifestyles that involved much greater reliance on marine produce, including fish, shellfish, and marine mammals such as seals and whales.

## Siberian hunters

The ancient settlement of Siberia has a complex history. Today, the Taiga Rescue Network, a nongovernmental network committed to "the protection, restoration and the sus-

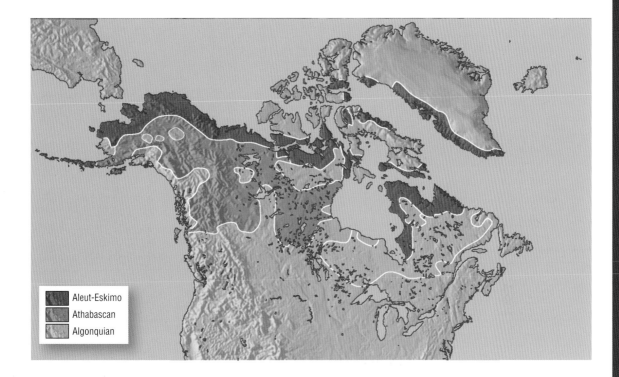

*The distribution of traditional linguistic groups in Canada*

tainable use of the boreal forest," recognizes 26 distinct native peoples living in the Siberian taiga. Most abundant are the Nenets (with more than 30,000 members) and least populous are the Oroks (fewer than 200). Many of today's native peoples settled in their current territories only within the last 2,000 years. In much of central and eastern Siberia, from the Yenisey River in the west to the Sea of Okhotsk in the east, many taiga peoples migrated between rivers in summer and dense taiga in winter.

The Evenki of western Siberia gathered in riverside settlements of 40–50 people in summer, and hunters spent about half their time fishing. In winter, the settlements disbanded and small groups of families roamed their hunting territories, staying only a few days in any one place. Regular movement provided fresh grazing for the reindeer, which served as both pack animals and riders' mounts. Shelters consisted of *chum,* conical huts made of wooden frames covered in birch bark or reindeer skins that could be quickly and easily dismantled and reassembled.

## Traditional codes of conduct

The traditional inhabitants of the taiga led a more or less nomadic lifestyle. Except for reindeer herders, who are found in Eurasia from about 2,000 years ago but do not have equivalents in North America, most taiga peoples relied on the natural economy of their landscape and did not take part in agricultural or stock-raising practices. They had no way of rapidly increasing animal and food production. If they used up the natural stocks of animals and plants in their traditional hunting, fishing, and gathering grounds and moved outside the area, they ran the risk of conflict with neighboring peoples.

Most anthropological studies of today's taiga peoples reveal traditional codes that govern conduct in exploiting the natural resources of the taiga. Such codes appear to help sustain resources so they are not exhausted. Common rules include the following:

- Do not kill more animals than you need.
- Do not catch young animals.
- Use all parts of a killed animal.
- Do not cut down young trees.
- Use dead, not live wood for firewood.

This practical concern for the conservation of natural resources was typically understood within a spiritual tradition. Traditional taiga peoples commonly see themselves as part of the natural environment—not separate from animals and plants. Animals have spirits and are to be revered. In a harsh landscape, where hardship is common and the possibility of starvation or death from exposure is present each winter, the human connection with the landscape and its plant and animal inhabitants is particularly strong.

The Algonquian peoples of eastern Siberia and the Khanty of western Siberia dug winter overnight shelters in the snow and covered the entrance with animal skins. Their quarry—often deer, but also a variety of furred animals, ranging from sable to bears—provided food and animal skins that could be traded or sold.

In the last few hundred years, many of eastern Siberia's peoples used dogs for pulling sleds and for tracking, attacking, or retrieving prey during the hunt. Since the 20th century, using skis for travel has almost entirely replaced riding on the backs of reindeer.

# Hunters and fishers

Many Khanty and Mansi peoples of western Siberia depended more on fishing than hunting. In winter, many families came together in well-established seasonal settlements of log huts where food was stored. From these communities of about 150 people, hunters and their families would leave for sorties (excursions) of a few days to bring back fresh meat. In summer, these larger communities disbanded, and the families would settle in groups of 10–15 people alongside a river which formed their fishing grounds. They chose sites for settlements where strong prevailing winds would reduce the nuisance from biting insects.

The Athabascan tribes of Alaska and western Canada combined hunting large land mammals, especially deer, with catching marine and freshwater fish and gathering shellfish. With the arrival of Europeans in the region in the 18th century, native peoples turned more to hunting animals for their fur, which could be traded or sold for European goods. Intensive hunting undoubtedly resulted in a massive decline in the numbers of many furred species and caused disruption to traditional communities who relocated to fresh hunting grounds (see "Overhunting," pages 144–146).

In North America, among the Algonquian peoples of the Labrador peninsula, such as the Cree and Ojibwa, hunting and fishing were of roughly equal importance. In winter, hunting was preferred, and in the summer, fishing. The lifestyle between mid-fall and mid-spring was nomadic, with several families in a group of about 50 people moving about their territory to find the best hunting grounds. In summer, the families came together in larger groups, settling close to the best fishing sites. However, the groups and their hunting or fishing approaches were fairly flexible. They adapted to the prevailing conditions and the changing seasons. They hunted waterfowl through the summer, turning more to deer in the autumn. If fishing proved poor in the summer, they would spend more time on hunting. In winter, if hunting was giving poor returns, they would turn to fishing. Traditionally, men were the hunters and fishers, with both women and men gathering nuts, roots, and wild fruits to complete the diet.

The Ojibwa, whose territory extended in a broad band north of Lake Superior, illustrate well how native peoples made best use of the plant and animal resources around them. Spruce trunks and thick branches provided poles for wigwams while thin branches were laid on the wigwam floor to provide a soft cushion on the hard ground. The spruce fragrance combined with the conifer needles acted as a deterrent to nuisance insects. The Ojibwa carved spruce wood into domestic utensils such as bowls. They used the bark of birch trees to cover wigwams, make baskets and cooking pots, and form the hull of canoes (see the sidebar). The oozing sap (resin) from trees was used as glue and boiled to make pitch as a waterproofing agent. Birch, cedar, or pine branches were fashioned into arrows with eagle, hawk, or turkey feathers tied to the shaft with sinew (tendon, the tough fibrous tissue that connects muscle to bone). Bows of ash, elm, or hemlock were strung with animal sinew. The Ojibwa constructed spears and knives from combinations of wood, stone, and bone. They sewed animal skins together to make well-insulating coats, mittens, and moccasins. Sometimes they elaborately embroidered them with moose hair and dyed threads or decorated them with floral or geometric designs created from porcupine quills. Such products form the basis for a continuing tradition of arts and crafts in traditional taiga communities today, with items sold to visitors vacationing in the region.

## The modern North American taiga

After the ancient colonization of the American continent, the first Europeans to arrive were probably Vikings who landed in Newfoundland in about 1000 C.E. They left the remains of a temporary settlement near present-day L'Anse-aux-Meadows.

The population mix of the North American taiga changed rapidly after the mid-1600s, when the French began settling in the St. Lawrence River valley and the British in the Hudson

## Using cedar and birch

In a land of limited resources, Native Americans of the Pacific coast used red cedar wood for building, transport, domestic utensils, and ceremonial objects. The wide range of cedar wood items included poles for dwellings, totem poles, dugout canoes, boxes and bowls, and ceremonial masks. Cedar bark they used as twine.

Native Americans of the Canadian northeast fashioned superb canoes from white birch, cedar, and spruce. Birch bark stretched over a cedar frame formed the hull, with the panels sewn into place using spruce roots as twine and seams made watertight with pine resin. These birch-bark canoes were incredibly light, allowing moose and caribou hunters to carry them over the landscape with ease.

Bay region. Many early colonizers began trading with the native taiga peoples. Soon outsiders began exploiting native communities and, through a variety of means, encouraged or forced natives to change their traditional ways of life. The French and British competed for the fur-rich territories of eastern Canada for more than a century, which finally led to a British-French colonial war. Between the 1750s and 1760s, this war waged on and off for more than seven years. Native Canadian groups fought on both sides. The last native taiga inhabitants to meet Europeans were tribes in the vicinity of Klondike, in southwest Yukon, during the gold rush of the 1890s.

Decades of hunting and trapping greatly depleted the populations of fur-bearing animals in central and eastern parts of North American boreal forest by the early 19th century. In 1840s Europe, fur clothes suddenly became less fashionable and the Canadian export market for furs dropped steeply. In the late 19th century, the Canadian government bought the land rights owned by the Hudson Bay Company and took legal control of hunting.

Since the 19th century, discoveries of rich mineral deposits have brought wealth to the taiga—but at a social and environmental cost. Gold was discovered in the bed of the Fraser River, British Columbia, in the late 1850s, prompting prospectors to

# Totems and totem poles

For many taiga peoples, forest animals are sacred, and some animals have special qualities that are particularly revered. In many cases, a tribal clan believes that it is descended from a particular animal, and this animal is the clan's emblem or totem. Killing a totem animal was against clan law.

Among many Athabascan tribes of eastern Siberia, Alaska, and northwest Canada, the wolf was the totem animal. Even if wolves were attacking a tribe's caribou or reindeer herds, it was forbidden to kill the predators. Doing so, it was believed, would incur the wrath of the spirit world and would bring more attacks by wolves.

Tribes in the American and Canadian Pacific northwest began making totem poles in the mid-18th century. Before then, they used stone tools that were inefficient at felling large trees. With the arrival of Europeans, iron tools became available. Native peoples traded their woven baskets, boxes, and fur pelts for iron axes, and the tradition of the totem pole soon followed.

Totem poles range from six feet (2 m) to 50 feet (15 m) tall. Skillfully carved and often brightly colored, they served a variety of purposes. Traditionally, the size and complexity of a family's totem pole demonstrated the family's status and history within the tribal community. A series of human and animal faces were often coupled with intricate geometric design. The poles usually depicted the family crest, showed family histories, honored the qualities of certain people and animals, and retold stories or legends. The pole also served to ward off evil spirits. Today, many totem poles are carved as souvenir sculptures.

*A totem pole made by the Haida people of Queen Charlotte Islands, British Columbia, Canada*

## Taiga medicine

Between them, taiga peoples traditionally used more than 1,000 plant species as their medicine store. Many soft fruits, including those of gooseberries, cowberries, and magnolia vines, are rich in vitamin C and contain stimulant chemicals that can stave off hunger and fatigue during long hunting expeditions. Many plant extracts have specific uses for treating particular conditions. Oils extracted from fir needles, such as those of the balsam fir, made effective antiseptics (they prevent wounds from becoming infected). Siberian peoples used the inner part of the bark of the larch as bandages. The Tanaina of Canada made teas from juniper branches and used them to treat several conditions, including pneumonia and tuberculosis. The Ojibwa used infusions of willow and Labrador tea plant to treat fevers. Berries of the swamp red currant were used to treat kidney stones. Sphagnum moss is both water-absorbent and antiseptic. Native North Americans found it to be a perfect natural diaper for babies.

In the Russian Far East, ginseng root extracts have long been prized for their stimulant and tonic properties, with a reputation for helping invigorate the body's natural healing abilities. The ginseng plant grows wild and is harvested each year from Russian forests. Such is the demand for ginseng in North America, Europe, and China, that it is increasingly grown in farms far away from the plant's place of origin.

arrive in the hundreds from the United States and other parts of Canada. Even greater gold discoveries were made in the 1880s and 1890s in Yukon Territory, culminating in the Klondike gold rush of the late 1890s, when thousands arrived to prospect in the Klondike River and its tributaries. The population of the nearby town of Dawson soon expanded from a few hundred to 16,000. In 1899, prospectors found more than U.S. $16 million of Klondike gold, but the rush collapsed almost as soon as it had begun. The rise and fall of towns whose existence depends upon a single exhaustible commodity is a common theme in the Canadian taiga (see "Mining," pages 139–142).

According to the Boreal Forest Network, a nongovernmental North American affiliate of the Taiga Rescue Network, about 80 percent of Canada's native people live in the taiga region. Some 30,000 Athabascan-speaking peoples live in the taiga of Alaska and northwest and central Canada. They include

Koyukon, Kutchin, Tana, Tanaina, and various Chippewa tribes that live in more or less traditional territories. Peoples of Inuit descent live to the north and in coastal regions of the northwest.

In central and eastern Canada live about 100,000 Algonquian speakers, the largest groups being the Cree and the Ojibwa. The Cree, for example, traditionally hunted caribou and moose, and in European colonial days, traded with both the British and the French.

Many North American taiga peoples no longer live in forested regions, and they have given up traditional ways of life. Many dwell in urban areas, living a more or less modern lifestyle. Some, particularly those inhabiting remote areas, continue to live a seminomadic way of life, combining hunting and fishing. Others live on reservations within the taiga region and carry on a semitraditional way of life, such as spending warmer months in tepees and wigwams. Some produce sculptures, jewelry, replicas of traditional artifacts, and other items for the tourist trade. Among native peoples who do not live in traditional communities or reservations, some still retain their ethnic identity through the clothes they wear, by practicing traditional arts and crafts, and by performing traditional dances and religious ceremonies.

## The modern Eurasian taiga

In today's Russian taiga, most people are descendants of those who entered the region since the late 1500s. In Siberia, most of these people arrived from Ukraine and the southern regions of Russia in a series of migrations. The settlers were escaping hardship in their original regions, and many cleared patches of land in the southern taiga and carried out subsistence farming. They lived, more or less peacefully, alongside the native peoples. Between the 1600s and 1800s, rising demand for fur in Russia and Europe encouraged hunters and trappers to go in search of the valuable fleeces of taiga animals such as the fox, beaver, mink, and sable. In 1840s Europe, when fur clothes abruptly went out of style, the lucrative Russian fur trade slumped.

During the 20th century, Siberia became a favored place for Russia governments to send criminals and people who disagreed with governments of the time. The tyrannical Soviet leader Joseph Stalin set up a system of forced labor camps in which countless thousands perished.

Today the descendants of native inhabitants are in the minority except in the Evenki Autonomous Okrug, a region of western Siberia where Evenki dominate. In Siberia, about two-thirds of people live in large cities such as Surgut, Irkutsk, Tomsk, and Yakutsk.

The Oroqen people live in the forested Heilongjiang province of northern China but within a few hundred miles of some of the most industrialized regions of China. Until recently, the Oroqen lived a nomadic, hunting lifestyle similar to that of eastern Siberian forest dwellers. They hunted deer and herded reindeer. In summer, they lived in birch bark–covered tents and in winter, in collapsible dwellings covered in deerskins. Today, many Oroqen live a settled lifestyle in dwellings supplied with electric power and with modern conveniences such as television and radio. Some Oroqen continue their traditional ways, wearing deerskin clothes and fur hats, with the men hunting deer on foot and horseback. Traditional Oroqen women still use birch bark to make canoes and fashion household items.

In Scandinavia and European Russia, some larger populations of taiga dwellers still maintain a more or less traditional lifestyle. In the taiga and tundra of Scandinavia and northeastern European Russia live more than 30,000 Sami (Lapps), many of whom still herd reindeer although many use modern practices. Some private landowners are challenging the Sami's customary right to live their nomadic reindeer-herding lifestyle. In Russia and Finland live about 100,000 Karelians, many of whom still earn most of their livelihood from hunting.

Since the breakup of the Soviet Union in 1991, Russian taiga peoples have been asserting their independence. They have created national and regional associations and some of the native groups have elected representatives on the Federal Assembly. While on the one hand, some native peoples are winning the fight to claim back traditional

*A reindeer herder resting with his family beside a river in Siberia, Russia* (Courtesy of Michio Hoshino/ Minden Pictures)

lands for hunting, fishing, and reindeer-raising, in other places commercialization and corruption have exploited native lands. In parts of western Siberia, for example, the Soviet government of the 1980s seized many traditional

Khanty territories to prospect for oil. Native peoples were forcibly relocated from their traditional hunting territories. Most are excluded from participation in the industrial development and now live in new villages where they no longer have forest territories to continue a more traditional way of life.

## Meeting today's challenges

Life in the taiga was traditionally tough. People had to be hardy to survive the cold winters on a restricted supply of food. Women typically gave birth by the campfire and often had only a few hours to recover before the family group moved on to the next hunting ground.

Even today, taiga life remains demanding. Some traditional peoples still live without benefit of modern medical facilities close at hand. In the Siberian taiga, the death rate for young babies in native communities remains about twice the Russian average.

From the 1600s, greater contact with outsiders brought new diseases to the taiga. Native peoples began succumbing to influenza, measles, tuberculosis, and smallpox—diseases to which they had little, if any, immunity. Colonizers also brought alcohol. Alcoholic beverages have never been a traditional part of taiga culture, and many taiga people lack the enzyme that rapidly breaks down alcohol in the body. For most taiga peoples, alcohol has an unusually powerful intoxicating effect.

Exploitation by outsiders, foreign diseases, and the introduction of alcohol and drugs are among the many challenges taiga peoples have had to face in the last few centuries. During the 19th century, Christian missionaries and national and regional authorities encouraged or forced native peoples to give up many of their traditional customs. In the 19th century, for example, both Canadian and United States governments banned potlatches, the tribal celebrations that accompany the setting up of a new totem pole (see the sidebar "Totems and totem poles," page 118). As a result, the tradition of totem pole carving almost died out. Authorities lifted the ban on potlatches only relatively recently—in the

1950s. Since the 1970s, many traditional communities have developed renewed fervor to protect their distinct language, values, and customs in their traditional territories.

The Ouje-Bougoumou Cree are the traditional inhabitants of a territory in northern Quebec. During the 20th century, mineral prospectors entered their homelands and created two nontraditional communities based on mining and forestry. The Cree were largely economically excluded from these communities.

Meanwhile, Ouje-Bougoumou Cree communities were being forcibly moved—seven times over a period of 50 years. In the early 1980s, the Cree community sought negotiations with the provincial government of Quebec for financial support toward the construction of a new village. They also sought to gain some degree of local jurisdiction over a portion of their traditional hunting territory. The Cree ultimately resorted to direct action, such as blockading roads and raised wider public awareness of their plight by establishing a traditional court in which they indicted the provincial and federal governments. This finally led to the Ouje-Bougoumou/Canada Agreement in May 1992, in which the federal government agreed to contribute financially to the cost of a new village. In ongoing negotiations the Cree are seeking to gain control over the natural resources of their traditional territory.

# CHAPTER 7

# USES OF THE TAIGA

As we have seen, the taiga is much more than the trees of its forest. It includes myriad microbes, animals, and smaller plants that live and grow on its trees, in the soil beneath, and in the rivers, lakes, and bogs that are widely scattered through the taiga. There are hundreds of resources that people can harvest sustainably from the taiga biome, some less obvious than others. For instance, trees provide wood pulp to make paper, timber for construction, and logs for burning as fuel, but less obviously they also yield resins for glues, fragrances, and medicines. The beauty of a forest—the shafts of light slanting through the tree canopy, the smell of pine in the air, and the majestic animals that wander through the undergrowth—give taiga forests a high amenity value for leisure and recreation. The taiga also has a hidden value—its so-called ecosystem functions (see the table "Some boreal-forest products and services," page 166). These include maintaining the quality of the air around us, preserving the cleanliness of water in lakes and rivers, and slowing runoff to prevent flooding (see the sidebar "Forests and freshwater," page 165).

Canada and Russia are the two countries with the largest expanses of taiga, and some statistics serve to highlight the diversity and importance of taiga products for their economies. In Canada, forestry is the second-largest industry (only agriculture is larger), and most of this activity occurs within the taiga. According to the FAO (the Food and Agriculture Organization of the United Nations), 74 percent of Canada's forest is boreal. Each year, Canadian companies employ more than 300,000 people to make forest products that bring in U.S. $50 billion in income. Many of Canada's mineral mines (not including petroleum oil, natural gas, stone, and gravel) are located in boreal forest regions. Canada is among the world's top five producers of aluminum, cadmium, copper, gold, platinum, silver, and uranium. In a single year, commercial fishers in Canada can take more than $100 million of freshwater fishes from Canada's lakes and rivers, most of which are found in taiga territory. In 2000, Canada's forests provided 16.4, 14.1, and 11.2 percent respectively of global production of sawn wood (lumber), pulp for paper, and industrial roundwood (stripped tree trunks).

According to FAO statistics, slightly more than 50 percent of Russia's land is forested, and of this, 86 percent is boreal forest. Russia's boreal forest accounts for just over 50 percent of the global area of coniferous forest. More than half of Russia's boreal forest is available for wood supply; the remainder is currently inaccessible for harvesting on a large scale because of lack of transport infrastructure. The Russian state owns all large forested areas, while harvesting of wood products on a large scale is almost entirely privatized. In 2000, Russia's forests—boreal and other—yielded 6.7, 4.7, and 3.1 percent respectively of global production of lumber, pulp for paper, and industrial roundwood. This reveals that Russia's forests are much less intensively harvested overall than those in Canada, although that does not necessarily mean that none of Russia's forests are currently overharvested. Also, this does not take into account the many non-wood resources that Russia's forests provide: wild fruits and berries, nuts and mushrooms, herbs and medicinal plants, tree resins, fodder and forage, fish and meat, and so on. Most of the boreal forest production—wood and other—is utilized within Russia. There is considerable scope for expansion for internal consumption as well as export.

## Hunting and fur farming

Among traditional taiga peoples, hunting was—and for some remains—a way of life. Animals provide food, and almost all of an animal carcass can be put to one use or another. Until the 16th century, hunting was sustainable in many parts of the taiga so that local animal populations were not depleted; the numbers taken were replaced by natural breeding. Since then, the situation in many taiga areas has changed dramatically (see "The modern North American taiga," pages 116–120, and "The modern Eurasian taiga," pages 120–123). One result was the creation of fur farms (see sidebar).

In most cases, hunting today is highly mechanized, with rifles and fast-moving vehicles replacing spears or bows and arrows and hunting on foot or reindeer-back. Nowadays, hunting is less likely to be for food than for the animal's fur pelt or the sport of the hunt.

In Canada today, for example, fur traders sell more than 100,000 beaver pelts and 2,000 brown bear pelts each year. The fur trade slumped dramatically in the 1970s, with environmental groups raising public awareness about the potential cruelty of hunting and trapping and promoting the use of alternatives to fur products. Demand fell for even the most prized fur pelt, that of the sable of the Siberian taiga (see the sidebar "Sable fur," page 128).

Although the number of fur pelts harvested each year in Canada has dropped from about 4 million in the late 1970s to 2 million in the early 2000s, the overall numbers harvested since then remain fairly stable. In 2001, the harvest of Canadian wildlife furs was worth more than $15 million, up 13 percent on the previous year.

## Fur farms

In the mid-1800s, with the decline in the supply of fur-bearing animals in the wild, fur farms—in which animals are bred for their fur pelts—began to be set up in Europe. European fur farmers raised stoats and sable and imported mink from North America to stock their farms. In Canada, the first fur farm was set up in 1887. European Russian fur farms did not become common until the 1950s, and Siberian fur farms are an even more recent innovation. In the early 2000s, more than two-thirds of Canada's fur pelts came from farmed animals, with mink, fox, and chinchilla being the most popular.

Fur farms exist both within and outside the taiga. Their impact upon the boreal forest has been twofold. On the one hand, they probably serve to lessen the pressure on hunting and trapping some of taiga's animals, notably stoat and sable. On the other hand, the escape of animals from fur farms releases exotic species into the wild, which compete with local wild species, as in the case of the mink in Eurasia.

## Sable fur

Sable is the most highly valued fur obtained by hunters in the taiga. In northern and central Siberia, the sable remains highly sought after. In the mid-20th century, the sable population declined due to a combination of factors, including overhunting. Since then, a breeding program that introduced sable back into the wild has helped the wild population recover such that hunting can be sustained. Today, a Siberian hunter pursuing sable with rifle in the early winter and with traps later in the season can take up to 100 sable a year. With the partial collapse of the European fur trade as a result of changing attitudes to wearing fur, however, sable is less in demand now and market prices for a sable coat remain fairly low. It is now more difficult for traditional hunters in Siberia to gain a living from selling to the fur trade.

Hunting and trapping are monitored at the provincial level in Canada, with each province issuing quotas and licenses to help ensure that the numbers harvested are sustainable. However, a report compiled for the Canadian Council of Forest Ministers (CCFM) in 2000 suggested that closer monitoring of animals in the wild, and pooling of data across provinces, was needed. This would allow population levels and threats to wildlife to be followed so that biologists and resource managers would have confidence in assessing whether a population was vulnerable, threatened, or endangered (see "Biodiversity," pages 169–172).

## Taiga tree products

Taiga trees yield a remarkably wide range of products, but the foremost product is wood, the dense, interior material of the tree trunk, roots, and branches. Many of wood's useful properties originate from the combination of thick-walled cells, glued together by natural substances such as lignin, that are arranged in parallel columns or cylinders to produce the grain of the wood.

It is useful to be reminded of the remarkable properties of wood that many of us take for granted. Most wood is exceptionally strong for its weight. It can be shaped using tools and readily fastened together with screws, nails, staples, adhesives, and other fixings. It is a good insulator against heat, sound, and electricity. It accepts paint, and it can be treated to resist rotting. Unlike most other materials used in the construction and furniture industries—materials such as plastics (usually made from petroleum oil products), metals, and cement—wood is renewable. Harvested in the correct way, wood can be grown to replace that which is cropped.

Despite major technological advances in the development of building materials and fuels in the 20th century, wood remains a vital resource. Many people still use timber from taiga conifers for building and furniture construction and logs as fuel for heating and cooking.

Conifers yield softwood, which is more pliable than most hardwood that comes from broad-leaved trees. Softwood's malleable nature comes from the abundance of wood fibers (narrow, tubular, hard-walled cells with pointed ends). Hardwoods have fewer fibers and more hard-walled, tubular cells of larger size.

Apart from its use as timber, softwood can be processed to make paper, cardboard, and composite woods such as chipboard. For making wood pulp—wood fibers suspended in water—conifers are easier to process than broad-leaved trees. Conifers have fewer knots and a looser grain, and their fibers are longer and more abundant, yielding stronger packaging products and newsprint (the paper on which newspapers are printed). While softwoods from conifers are generally not as strong as hardwoods from broad-leaved trees, they grow faster and form pure stands with trees of similar size, so they are easier to harvest. This drives down costs, which means softwoods can be sold at comparatively low prices.

Conifer trunks tend to grow fairly straight and usually have long sections with relatively few knots where branches emerge. This makes them particularly useful as sources of roundwood and lumber.

Roundwood is tree trunk stripped of its bark. Dried and then treated with preservatives to prevent decay and attack by insect pests, roundwood provides posts, poles, and pilings. Posts are generally less than four inches (10 cm) across and are used as vertical supports in fences. Poles are longer and thicker and are often used for supporting telephone or power lines. In the days of sail, the tall, straight roundwood of conifers was favored for ships' masts, and some foresters still call old-growth pine forests "naval forests." The thickest roundwood timbers of all are pilings, used to support some buildings as well as structures in water, such as wharves. In Siberia, the larch—with its dense, resinous, almost rot-proof wood—is favored for the pilings of buildings in permafrost areas and in waterlogged soils. Larch is so dense that it sinks in water. Foresters need to counterbalance larch with more buoyant woods when floating logs downriver.

Lumber refers to the planks and other large pieces of wood formed when trunks are cut into strips. The construction industry uses lumber for a wide range of frames, supports, and panels. In Siberia, the aboveground parts of many houses are constructed of Siberian pine, which remains intact for hundreds of years. In North America and Eurasia, manufacturers use heavy lumber for railroad ties. In the 19th century, railroads advanced over Canada and northern United States on ties made of American larch (tamarack), another taiga tree. Lumber is also used in the packaging and furniture industries. Finer pieces of lumber are fashioned into parts of toys, sporting goods, and countless other products. Conifer wood is also cut into thin sheets called veneers. They can be used as attractive covering layers on poorer-quality construction material or shaped to make small practical items such as baskets, tongue depressors, matches, and toothpicks.

Manufacturers create many wood products by combining wood with other materials to take advantage of the best properties of each. These products are called wood-based composites. Plywood and particleboard are made by combining wood with adhesive resins. In plywood, several sheets of veneer, with their grains arranged at right angles, are glued together. This creates material that is less likely than conventional lumber to shrink, swell, distort, or split. Particleboard, as its name suggests, is made from wood particles. These are by-products—in the form of sawdust, shavings, flakes, and so on—produced by taiga sawmills and paper mills (See "The timber, pulp, and paper industries," pages 130–133). Particleboard, created by pressing the wood particles together with adhesive at high temperature and pressure, is usually less strong than plywood.

Much finer than wood particles, wood fibers are extracted using chemical or mechanical processes. They are then reconstituted in various forms to generate a wide range of products from paper to insulation board. In making paper or paperboard, wood pulp is sieved to produce a mat of fibers that is drained, compressed, and dried to produce paper. Insulation board is formed by lightly compressing a much thicker layer of wood fibers. Large boards or panels create a heat-insulating or a sound-proofing layer. Medium-density fiberboard (MDF) and hardboard are also fiber-based products. Hardboard contains fibers bound together by lignin, the natural organic substance that bonds wood fibers and vessels together in trees. Hardboard is commonly used for making thin panels. In the case of MDF, fibers or bundles of fibers are bonded with adhesive. MDF combines many of the best properties of composite wood materials and is rapidly replacing plywood or particleboard for making low-cost furniture, fixtures, and fittings.

## The timber, pulp, and paper industries

Large-scale clear-cutting of taiga forest in Scandinavia and northwest Russia began some 500 years ago to provide wood to build ships for major European powers, especially the Netherlands and Britain. Timber merchants transported the tree trunks downriver to ports in the Baltic Sea, and from there by boat to North Sea shipyards.

From the 1600s, loggers in Sweden and Finland also felled trees to provide fuel for the iron industry. Today, little of the original Scandinavian taiga forest remains. The European Russian taiga has retained more area of old-growth coniferous forest than the rest of Europe put together. The Taiga Rescue Network, a network of nongovernmental organizations, including representatives of indigenous peoples that promote sensitive development of the taiga region, is pressing for these Russian old-growth forests to be designated as areas protected from forestry and mining operations.

In Canada, large-scale logging of the taiga forest did not begin until the early 19th century. In southeast Canada, pine timber was in demand for props, planks, ships' masts, and staves (curved planks) for barrels. By 1850, Britain was receiving more than two-thirds of Canada's forestry products, with most of the rest going to the United States. By 1860, foresters had cut down almost all the pines in New Brunswick. Tree felling shifted inland. Most of the inland timber came from river valleys because the only easy way to transport logs was to float them downstream. As one area after another was cleared of trees, developers assumed that the cleared land would no longer produce timber and should be taken over for agriculture. However, by the 1870s, the Canadians were learning from the Scandinavian experience that, given the right circumstances, cleared pine forests could regrow. Conifers were a renewable resource.

In the mid-1880s, a railroad connection was established between the Pacific coast and the Great Lakes region. Timber could now be transported long distances by rail rather than by river. At about that time, paper production grew in importance. Canadians began building large pulp- and paper-producing factories, and the exploitation of conifer forests extended farther north and west. In the 1920s, the

## Christmas trees

In North America and Europe, people buy conifer trees to decorate their homes at Christmas. The tradition can be traced back to Germany in about 1,000 C.E. According to legend, St. Boniface discovered pagans worshipping an oak tree, and in his anger he cut the tree down. A fir tree sprang up in its place, which he took as a positive sign from God. So a tradition was begun linking fir trees with Christian worship.

In the United States alone, about 35 million Christmas tree conifers are sold each year, with Scotch pine as the favorite. In Europe, Norway spruce is popular. Most Christmas trees are grown in plantations and harvested at six to seven feet (about 2 m) tall, when they are six to 10 years old. Growing them in plantations—often outside taiga regions—reduces pressure on obtaining the trees from the taiga itself.

United States lifted the import tariff on newsprint, and the Canadian pulp and paper industry found a new market. Today, Canada produces more than one-quarter of the world's newsprint, with most of it exported to the United States.

Paper and packaging products are not the only uses for pulp. Cellulose, a complex sugar and the main chemical ingredient in wood fibers, can be chemically converted into a variety of useful products. Cellulose derivatives such as cellulose nitrate and cellulose acetate are ingredients in glues, plastics, and even explosives. Textile manufacturers process cellulose to make rayon and acetate fabrics, which are widely used in the upholstery and clothing industries.

## Forestry

Forest ecology professor Hamish Kimmins, in the 1997 edition of his book *Balancing Act,* defines forestry as "the art, science, and practice of managing forested landscapes to provide a sustained production of a variety of goods and services for society." Forestry in many of today's boreal regions takes into account that a given forest area serves many purposes. It provides non-wood products such as resins; food supplies such as meat and fish; recreational services such as walking, fishing, shooting, and skiing; and ecosystem services such as soil conservation, watershed management, and wildlife protection. This means that forestry today tends to operate according to "ecosystem" management principles.

*Silviculture,* a major arm of forestry, is the planting, tending, and harvesting of trees. If a forest is to be managed so that a sustained yield of wood can be harvested from a given area at regular intervals, then the rate at which wood is removed must be counterbalanced by tree growth. For example, imagine a forest manager who is responsible for gaining a sustained yield of wood from a 400-acre (160-ha) stand of pine trees in Finland. Other factors aside, if each year-class of trees in the age range of one to 40 covers 10 acres of the forest, and the trees are harvested when 40 years old, then the manager ought to be able to sustainably harvest 10 acres of forest each year. This could be continued into the foreseeable future, assuming the clear-cut forest is reseeded or replanted appropriately (see "Assisting forest regeneration," pages 178–179).

The cutting cycle, or *rotation*—the time between planting and harvesting—depends on the species of tree and its intended use. The rotation for Scotch pine or Douglas fir to be used as roundwood or lumber may be as much as 100 years. For pine trees to be used as wood pulp, the rotation is typically about 30–40 years. As is clear from these rotations, modern forestry usually operates according to management plans that extend many decades into the future. Managers employ one of two main methods for harvesting: clear-cutting and selective cutting.

*Clear-cutting* in its purest form—with all sizable trees cut down in a given area—is best employed on even-age stands of trees, composed of one or two species, which have seedlings that can grow in bright sunlight. It is an effective means for regenerating stands of high-value species such as Scotch pine and Douglas fir that require absence of shade to grow well. Clear-cutting is a quick and efficient method of harvesting if a high economic return from a forest stand is required in a short space of time. It allows diseased or pest insect–infested forest to be surgically removed, and it offers the potential for regenerating the forest with genetically "improved" stock (see "Maintaining genetic diversity," pages 174–176).

Clear-cutting is criticized on several counts. First, it tends to replace mixed-age stands of trees with single-age stands. In the early stages of recovery, clear-cutting temporarily reduces the diversity of the biological community in the cleared area (see "Biodiversity," pages 169–172). If the clear-cut area is replaced with a stand of trees of largely one or two species and these are of the same age, then the entire stand is vulnerable to a potentially destructive environmental shift. A factor that negatively affects one tree—be it disease, an insect pest, or fire—may well affect all.

Second, clear-cutting leaves large open spaces that reduce protection from storms for those trees living alongside the clear-cut area. And by removing much of the vegetation that encourages water storage in the soil and impedes water flow, clear-cutting tends to encourage surface runoff and increase soil erosion on sloping land. This adds higher levels of sediment to watercourses downstream of the clear-cut, with a variety of effects, including changes in water quality and potential blockage or diversion of stream channels (see the sidebar "Forests and freshwater," page 165).

Clear-cutting also has the potential to create a fire risk, but this depends upon the method of clear-cutting and the state of the land left behind. If loggers leave large amounts of debris in their wake—logs, broken branches, loose bark, and sawdust—then this tinder, along with the lack of humidity in the microclimate of the cleared region, creates an increased fire risk in dry weather.

Finally, in many people's perception, clear-cutting scars the landscape, reducing its scenic beauty and its recreational amenity value. But as we shall see later, the benefits or otherwise of clear-cutting is very dependent on context, and the way in which the clear-cutting is carried out (see "Fragmentation," pages 148–149, and "Tree harvesting," pages 176–178).

Modifications of clear-cutting include the *seed-tree method,* in which most of the mature trees are removed in a single cut, but some are left standing to supply seed for the new stand. The *shelterwood method* involves removing many of the mature trees but leaving enough standing to supply seed and to shade between 30 and 80 percent of the ground so that shade-favoring seedlings can grow in subsequent years. Once the new growth of trees is several years old, the mature trees left standing are harvested. *Strip cutting* involves clear-cutting strips of forest that are typically about 250 feet (80 m) wide. The clear-cut strips benefit from the surrounding trees acting as seed sources. Such strips are also less likely to cause excessive runoff, soil erosion, and nutrient depletion than large clear-cut patches that are roughly square or circular.

*Selective cutting* is a much more hunt-and-pick method than modified forms of clear-cutting. Mature trees of economically favored species are picked out and removed from the forest a few at a time in an ongoing rotation, with selective tree removal typically at five- to 10-year intervals. "Trash species" and deformed trees are also selectively removed.

## Annual allowable cut

The annual allowable cut (AAC) is a calculation of the permissible rate of harvest of eco-nomically important trees from a forest in a given year. The calculation of AACs is highly controversial. The methods for calculating AACs vary from country to country and even province to province. AAC calculation methods also vary depending on whether the crop-ping is single-species or multispecies and whether a single-age or multiage stand is required. AACs also take into account economic considerations, such as the prevailing demand for a particular type of wood product. At its simplest, an AAC could be calculated based on the annual tree harvest being replaced by tree growth, in a simple rotation, but such circumstances rarely apply. Depending on situation, AACs should allow for sustain-able management of the forest over many decades while also ensuring nontimber values are maintained.

Such selective removal is the favored method of harvesting in many of the mixed conifer and broad-leaved forests that characterize the southern taiga (see "Where is taiga?" pages 2–4). Selective cutting works particularly well for harvesting shade-loving species.

## Agriculture

Taiga country, with its thin soils and short growing season, is poor for cultivating agricultural crops and raising livestock such as cattle and sheep. Most farm animals cannot survive the cold taiga winters unless the stock holders bring in addi-tional food to feed them and keep them in shelters. In some localities, sheep and cattle can be fed with hay cut from local meadows close to rivers, but such stock-raising is always a small-scale operation.

People of the Eurasian taiga have raised reindeer for many centuries. The reindeer can survive during the winter feeding on lichens, berries, and mushrooms that they dig from beneath the snow. For the Evenki people of eastern Siberia, reindeer serve as pack animals and provide milk. Among the reindeer-herding Nenet people of eastern Siberia, almost every part of a reindeer carcass has a use. Each family looks after a herd of about 70–100 animals. When a reindeer is slaughtered, the Nenet drink the blood and cook or store the meat. They use reindeer fat for cooking, lighting fuel, and waterproofing. Reindeer skin is made into shoes and clothes, while the sinews and tendons make sewing threads. Finally, Nenet carve reindeer antlers into useful tools or attractive decorations.

Growing vegetables and cereals is a tradition stretching back at least several hundred years among some taiga peoples, particularly in Eurasia. Small plots are cleared for growing vegetables such as carrots, onions, and turnips. Wheat and rye for bread-making are grown in fields close to rivers. Bread and vegetables make a welcome addition to the meat- and fish-rich taiga diet. Relatively little taiga forest has been cleared for these practices, and those that are often revert back to forest in time.

Of much greater significance is the removal of forest to clear room for mixed farming at the southern edge of the taiga. In British Columbia and Alberta, for example, large areas of spruce and aspen forest have been cleared for agriculture. Where trees once stood now grow cereals, oilseed rape to make vegetable oils, fodder plants for cattle feed, and a variety of vegetables. In central Canadian provinces, many farmers raise cattle that graze on grasses beneath thin forests of aspen and poplar. The farmers clear some of the forest for growing cereals as cattle feed. In southern Ontario and Quebec, the milder climate favors farmers growing clover, potatoes, and even corn. In North America and Russia, there is continuing pressure to convert the southern taiga to agriculture.

Gathering plant and fungal produce—wild fruits, nuts, mushrooms, herbs, and medicinal plants—is widely practiced in taiga regions, and is a significant contributor to local subsistence economies (see "The mixed economy," pages 142–143).

## Hydroelectric power

Modern hydroelectric plants, also called water power or hydropower plants, usually employ cascading water to turn the blades of a turbine. The rotating turbine shaft, in turn, rotates coils within a generator that produces electricity. To be commercially viable, hydroelectric schemes require large volumes of water dropping down sizable slopes. Taiga regions that are hilly or mountainous and have firm ground can make good sites for hydroelectric plants. One of the world's largest hydroelectric systems, the James Bay complex in Canada, is sited in taiga territory. In Canada, more than 50 percent of the nation's electricity is generated by hydropower—most of it within taiga regions. In Norway, hydropower accounts for more than 90 percent of electricity production.

Large hydroelectric systems generally involve damming the river to hold back the water and control the water flow though pipes to drive turbines. Small plants may not involve dams but instead rely on the natural flow of the river.

Large-scale hydroelectric systems have many advantages as sources of electricity. Although initial construction costs are high, and building a dam and generating system may take five years or more, once completed the system has a long life. After construction, such schemes produce little obvious pollution, and they have low operating costs. They are a safe and reliable source of electrical power. Once operating, they produce electricity at relatively low cost. However, many hydroelectric projects—particularly large plants—are much more disruptive of the environment and have greater impact on the lives of people in the locality than early estimates suggested (see "Hydroelectricity," pages 151–153). There are moves to reduce the size of new hydroelectric systems in an effort to minimize negative effects.

## Fishing

Taiga territory—in many places underlain by hard, ancient rock formations—contains more lakes than any other biome. More than 1 million lakes exist across the taiga biome, ranging in size from ponds of a few acres to central Siberia's Lake Baikal, which contains 18 percent of Earth's liquid freshwater.

Because they lie on hard rock, many taiga lakes and rivers contain relatively few dissolved nutrients. Coupled with the fact that they lie in cold climates where the growing season is short, their waters support fairly small populations of phyto-plankton (microscopic floating plants) and other aquatic plants. Because there is such low plant productivity, the populations of invertebrates and fish higher up the food chain are small too. So, most taiga waters do not contain large populations of fish. A lake of a few acres may contain only a few hundred pan-size fish. A family of anglers taking 10 such fish in a day may be removing 2 percent or more of the lake's sizable fish. A few weeks worth of fishing would be enough to severely deplete the lake's stock. Consequently, many of the taiga's lakes—now much more accessible because of improvements in transport methods, from snowmobiles to aircraft—have already been overfished.

There are exceptions to this low productivity. Many taiga rivers receive an annual influx of migrating salmon that have grown fat at sea and are swimming upriver to spawn. Some of Russia's rivers have a run of sturgeon that swim upriver from coastal waters to breed. North America's great taiga lakes, extending in a belt from Great Bear Lake in the north to Lake Superior in the south, are more productive than typical taiga lakes. They receive dissolved nutrients from sedimentary rocks and support more plant life and, in turn, larger fish populations.

Taiga fish—particularly sturgeon and members of the salmon family—have good flavor and command high prices. Sport-fishing permits for catching these fish can be a valuable source of revenue for managers of taiga's lakes and rivers.

Where commercial fishing with nets has been carried out on a large scale, the fish stock tends to be depleted fairly quickly unless artificial restocking is carried out. Between 1930 and 1960 in the Tyumen region of western Siberia, the fish catch from rivers increased from some 18,000 U.S. tons (16,500 tonnes) to 23,000 U.S. tons (21,000 tonnes) a year. It then fell to about 10,500 U.S. tons (9,500 tonnes) by the late 1980s. Overfishing, water pollution, and new dams (which block the migration of spawning fish) were blamed for the collapse.

## Mining

Beneath boreal forests lie extractable deposits of high-value metals such as iron, zinc, chromium, nickel, uranium, gold, and silver. Exploiting such deposits entails forest clearance, extensive excavation, and accompanying infrastructure such as transport links and accommodation facilities. Mining developments tend to cause considerable disturbance to taiga ecosystems, ranging from scarring of the landscape to sedimentation and metal pollution of local streams and forest fragmentation caused by cutting transport corridors. Mining opens up access to remote forest areas for other developments such as logging and hydroelectric power generation.

The demand for metals on the international market is quite fickle, and well-established mines commonly go into decline and become nonviable within 20 years. Restoring an area to a forest cover similar to that which existed before excavation is costly. In Canada, mining companies sign "closure and remediation" contracts agreeing to decommission the mine and provide some form of land reclamation. Undertaking such remediation work is highly expensive and may require the mine and its surroundings to be maintained and serviced long after the operation closes. All in all, mining activities have considerable impact on localized regions of the taiga biome, and the land and water in their locality is unlikely to ever provide the same quality of ecosystem services it provided before development took place.

The Shield Region of Canada's taiga is one of the world's richest sources of metals. The first major discoveries were made when strips of forest were cleared and soil excavated to lay railroad. In the late 19th century, surface veins of high-quality silver were found near Cobalt, Ontario, and by the 1910s, Cobalt was a thriving mining community, with a population greater than 5,000. Larger towns became established nearby when gold and then copper deposits were found.

Mines and the nearby towns that grow in their wake often follow a boom-and-bust cycle. After mineral deposits are discovered, excavation gradually builds and reaches a peak, and then the deposits gradually become exhausted or else the market demand for the mineral falls off and the mines become unprofitable. The once-thriving mining towns fall into decline. This has happened time and again in the Canadian taiga. Sometimes the cycle is repeated several times in the same locality, as minerals that once fell in price become in demand again and worth excavating. The uranium deposits of northwest Saskatchewan offer a clear example. The fortunes of nearby Uranium City have risen and fallen with fluctuations in the value of uranium on the international market. At its peak, Uranium City had a population of more than 5,000, but in the late 1990s its population fell to about 200 (see sidebar). To avoid the economic and social problems associated with the rise and fall of single-commodity towns, it has become common practice for miners to be transported into the mining site—often by plane—rather than housed in towns established locally.

During the mid-20th century, Western countries imposed a boycott on exports to the Soviet Union. This led Russian prospectors to hunt for mineral resources all over Russia. In the mid-1950s a young geologist, Larissa Popugayeva, found Russia's first major diamond deposits in Siberia. Further discoveries in the Lena Basin of central Siberia led to the growth of the city of Mirnyy as Russia's diamond capital. By 2000, a

## Uranium City

The growth of the nuclear weapons industry in the early 1950s led to the construction of northern Saskatchewan's Uranium City in the mid-1950s. The provincial government funded the town's construction to provide housing and other services to workers in nearby uranium mines and uranium-processing plants. In the early 1960s, with the collapse in demand for uranium for military purposes (uranium deposits had also been found in other countries) Uranium City declined. The mining community was in danger of becoming a ghost town.

By the late 1960s, the demand for uranium took an upturn, as countries across the world began to develop nuclear-based power industries. Uranium City began to prosper again and prosperity continued until the 1970s, by which time the nearby higher-grade uranium deposits were becoming exhausted and the international price of uranium had once again fallen. Uranium City fell into decline once more. As of the 1990s Uranium City, with its hospital and other services built for a thriving community, had only about 200 inhabitants. Geologists, mineral prospectors, and sports anglers were among the few outsiders who visited.

labor force of about 40,000 in this region was producing some $1.6 billion in diamonds—about one-quarter of the global market. Some other sectors of Russia's mining industries have fared less well. In 2003, with much of Russia's subsidized mining industries sold to private companies who initiated downsizing, the World Bank was backing a scheme to relocate 600,000 people from remote Siberian and Arctic lands to Moscow.

## The mixed economy

In the taiga, two economies exist side by side. The formal economy is one where people go to work and obtain a regular wage; this is the prevalent economy in North America and Europe. The informal economy is a subsistence one, where people live off the land and trade goods and services with each other with or without cash changing hands. The subsistence economy existed long before the formal one, and it remains important in most taiga regions. Because information about the informal economy is difficult to gather and quantify, however, it is left out of many government statistics, and its importance is often undervalued. But one recent study in Canada highlighted its significance.

In the 1990s, the Canadian government sponsored a task force called Yukon 2000 to investigate the Yukon's future economic development. Part of the analysis revealed the importance of so-called country foods. These are wild foods harvested from the locality, such as meat and fish from hunting and fishing and berries, vegetables, and mushrooms collected from the forests, hedges, and meadows. Included, too, are candies, preserves, and alcoholic beverages made from natural products, such as birch syrup, cloudberry preserve, and berry wines. Altogether, country foods contributed more than U.S. $7 million each year to the Yukon's economy.

The informal economy—involving bartering and exchanging skills—includes many house-building and household maintenance services that wage earners elsewhere purchase. People in the local community help each other build their houses, install their plumbing and electricity, and decorate their properties. The subsistence economy involves people trading goods, such as wood fuel, for services, such as boiler maintenance. The informal economy thrives, yet it is often underestimated in plans set by government officials, economists, and resource managers. The subsistence economy is the lifeblood of local taiga communities but can be destroyed by the large-scale, quick-profit activities of corporations and governments.

In conclusion, the taiga offers a rich variety of resources. It provides many ecosystem services, although the economic benefits of these are often overlooked, and many of the beneficiaries live outside the boreal forest region. Some activities—such as hunting, gathering, and forestry—are sustainable if properly managed, while mining activities tend to offer short-term gain at the expense of long-term environmental disruption. Balancing the exploitation of taiga's resources in a given locality requires an understanding of the potential negative impacts posed by each type of development. This is considered in chapter 8.

# THREATS TO THE TAIGA

When Europeans began colonizing North America in the 1500s, they described a landscape teeming with life. However, the North American landscape was not an untouched one. The native peoples who had lived there for thousands of years had already shaped the landscape dramatically. The myth of the "noble savage" who walks lightly upon the Earth, leaving it unaltered, is an overstated one. Through their hunting, the early inhabitants of North America probably helped drive at least 20 species of large mammal to extinction, ranging from mammoths and sloths to antelope and oxen. However, once Europeans arrived, the new colonizers managed to wreak more havoc on the environment in 400 years than earlier human invasions had managed in the previous 10,000.

## Overhunting

The European colonizers famously overhunted North American animals. In the 1600s, some French fur trappers operating in eastern Canada were setting 100–200 traps at a time instead of the 20–60 native hunters set. In the 1700s, the Hudson Bay Company, operated by the English, and the North West Company, set up by the Scots, competed with one another to buy as many furs as Native Americans could provide. By the late 1700s, the extermination of populations of fur-bearing animals in traditional hunting grounds meant that many groups of Cree and Ojibwa had to relocate to practice their traditional way of life. Such upheavals triggered fighting between native groups. Likewise, deer and bison—the main traditional sources of meat—had become scarce, and this forced changes in native peoples' diets and their way of hunting.

In the 1870s, the Canadian government took over legal control of hunting in the taiga, but the numbers of fur-bearing animals today probably bear little resemblance to the balance that existed before the 1600s. Otters and martens, for example, are much scarcer today, but this is due to environmental changes as well as past overhunting.

In Siberia, with the arrival of Russians from the south beginning in the 1500s, native Siberians began to hunt animals to provide meat and fur to sell or trade, rather than only for their own needs. Coupled with the use of firearms which replaced traditional weapons, this new approach greatly increased the hunting pressure on taiga animals. Beaver and sable—with their highly prized fur—became scarce in Europe and western Siberia by the late 1700s. Also highly prized in Europe and Asia were deer antlers, valued for their supposed medicinal properties when ground into a powder and added to potions. By the 1800s, the number of deer in the more accessible Eurasian taiga forests had declined dramatically too.

In the 20th century, the use of fast-moving vehicles such as snowmobiles has opened up regions of the taiga previously inaccessible to hunters. Hunters can cover much more ground in a single day than they could by traditional means of transport, such as ski or dogsled. By the 1960s, teams of hunters using snowmobiles were catching 3,000 sable in a year, and by the 1980s, the sable had become

## Habitat change, habitat loss

Habitat change and habitat loss are not quite the same thing, although over the span of a few decades, they appear to be the same. Strictly, habitat loss is the removal of a community of organisms that will never again be reinstated. This could occur where an area of forest is cleared for agriculture or for building houses. For all intents and purposes, the forest will never again reestablish, and the original habitat has been lost. If the forest were clear-cut, however, and allowed to reestablish—a process that might take more than 100 years before succession results in a similar assemblage to that already there—then this can be regarded as habitat change.

threatened over much of its former stronghold in central and eastern Siberia.

Hunting can be managed so as to complement forestry management, as currently takes place in many parts of Canada, Finland, Norway, and Sweden. For example, moose (elk) and caribou (reindeer) populations are harvested, often under a permit scheme whereby numbers taken are regulated. Moose consume saplings and strip the bark from mature trees, so they can be perceived as a pest by foresters. If hunted in carefully regulated numbers, moose can provide a bonus income by providing meat or offering sport hunting for vacationers as part of a "wilderness" experience. However, even regulated hunting could have unexpected impacts on other species (see "Endangered species in Canada's taiga," pages 172–174). Ideally, hunting should be regulated and restrictions enforced according to best practices based on scientific monitoring.

## Clear-cutting

Clear-cutting or clear-felling—where almost all the trees in a given area are cut down—is still a common forestry practice and is responsible for much loss or change of taiga habitat (see sidebar). In Canada in the mid-1990s, clear-cutting accounted for about 90 percent of the country's harvested timber. Canadian clear-cuts range in size from a few tens of acres to several thousand. Sometimes, very few shrubs or small trees are left standing. Prospectors may use heavy vehicles to drag away the fallen trees. Doing so compacts the earth and damages shrubs and ground-level vegetation. In other instances, prospectors take care to leave as much shrub and ground cover as possible. Once the trees are removed, some prospectors allow the cleared site to recover more or less naturally. Others lightly dig over the soil and seed the ground, or more intensively dig the ground, apply weed-killers, and plant young trees.

Clear-cutting to harvest wood and then encouraging regrowth invariably results in "old-growth" forest being replaced by "middle-age" forest. Old-growth forest contains trees of different ages. This includes old and decayed ones plus young trees that have grown in clearings created when old or diseased trees have fallen. Such forests contain a wide range of microhabitats that, in turn, support a diverse range of animals and plants (see "Biodiversity," pages 169–172).

Forests that are harvested on a regular basis for their wood are often managed intensively, such that the forest becomes dominated by only one species of trees, and these trees are encouraged to grow to the same age and height before they are harvested. These forests are much less biodiverse than old-growth woodland. Tree growth slows when trees become old, so timber farmers harvest the trees when they are still growing fast—in their middle age. A forestry industry driven by profits is rarely interested in preserving old-growth forest.

Clear-cutting is sometimes compared to fire as a way in which forest is cleared and subsequently renews itself. Both fire and clear-cutting increase the soil's susceptibility to weathering and nutrient loss. But, just as fires can vary in size and intensity, so can clear-cutting, so simple comparisons are not easy.

Clear-cutting has clear advantages for timber harvesters, but it is also of benefit to some forms of wildlife, especially those that thrive near forest edges or in clearings. On balance, however, clear-cutting is much more criticized than it is praised. Unless care is taken to leave plenty of ground cover, the soil becomes more liable to erosion. After rainfall, water flows off the land taking soil and nutrients with it. Soils become impoverished, and local streams and rivers may become polluted by the runoff.

Forestry policies and practices are gradually changing. In places, clear-cutting is gradually making way to strip-cutting, selective felling, or harvesting using the shelterwood method (see "Forestry," pages 133–136), leaving a more mixed-forest environment, both in terms of tree species and their ages. As the benefits of a mixed-age forest for multiple use become more apparent, its cultivation is gradually becoming a more acceptable practice. Where clear-cutting continues, the trend is to leave more ground cover to help preserve the soil and to maintain habitats for wildlife. Clear-cut areas are becoming smaller and less uniform in shape, and they are being planned with more

## The Great Bear Rainforest

The temperate forests that extend along the Pacific coast from Oregon to Alaska have sufficiently high rainfall to be classed as "rain forest." In the last 30 years, forestry companies have reduced the area of rain forest to about half. The Great Bear Rainforest of British Columbia is the largest remaining expanse. It is a stronghold for about 2,000 grizzly bears, its rivers harbor five species of salmon in all, and the forest contains thousand-year-old conifer trees valued at more than $25,000 each. Environmental organizations continue to campaign to conserve the remaining forest and to prevent timber removal by clear-cutting.

consideration for maintaining biodiversity. Planned clear-cutting—by providing small clearings in the forest—can actually be used as a strategy to maintain biodiversity rather than diminish it.

## Fragmentation

As we have seen, clear-cutting parts of a forest can have impact much greater than the area of forest removed would suggest. The process of carving up a forest into isolated units of woodland is called *fragmentation.*

If tracts are cut through a forest, these passages can vastly increase the number of "forest edges"—a different habitat from the dense forest itself. Many forest animals are reluctant to travel across open ground, particularly if people regularly cross this ground. Human disturbance to wildlife drops off rapidly with increasing distances from roads. Canadian land-use planners regard the forest within about 1,100 yards (1 km) of a road as disturbed from the point of view of wildlife. In British Columbia, nearly one-quarter of the landscape is within this distance of a road; about three-quarters is regarded as undisturbed. However, bird species that live in the deep forest may not flourish in small fragments of forest, even if most of the fragment is at least 1,100 yards from a road. Forest-edge species may compete aggressively with them for food, and the breeding success of forest-interior species is compromised.

Researchers have discovered that forest wolves are rarely found where the length of road is greater than 1,300 yards per square mile (equivalent to 450 m/km$^2$). Much of the Canadian taiga is well below this level, but where new developments occur, the situation can change rapidly and dramatically.

Evidence from studies in mixed temperate forests reveals that fragmentation can reduce nesting success among songbirds because nests are more visible and accessible to predators, which feed on eggs or hatchlings. In the tropical rain forest of the Amazon, recent research reveals that small fragments of forest contain a biased subset of the original flora and fauna that was adapted to life in larger stands. For example, small stands contain more light-loving species and fewer understory species. Similar observations might soon be forthcoming for boreal forests.

For plants and animals that cannot easily disperse from one forest stand to another, the fragmentation of the forest habitat can reduce the original large interbreeding population to numerous smaller populations that do not interbreed. The smaller populations are liable to inbreeding, in which individuals breed with others that have very similar genetic constitutions. In such circumstances, individuals are more likely to receive a double dose of harmful genes (one from each parent). This reduces the viability of the offspring. Also, because there is reduced genetic variability among the population as a whole, there is a smaller range of genetic constitutions on which natural selection can act. If an adverse event, such as the arrival of a virulent disease organism, affects one individual, it is likely that most or all of the other individuals will be affected too. The population could die out. Other factors aside, separate small populations in a geographic region may be more liable to extinction than a large interbreeding population inhabiting the same overall area.

## Fires

Natural, lightning-caused fires are widespread in conifer forests. In North America, intense fires that burn large areas of forest have occurred regularly. By studying tree growth rings and the charred remains in woodland soil deposits, scientists have discovered that widespread forest fires occur once every 50–200 years on average, depending on location.

In Canada, intense, widespread forest fires are becoming more common. One reason is climate change. Since the 1990s, some summers in parts of the North American taiga have become much warmer and drier than the average of recent decades. This creates conditions with plenty of dry tinder—dead branches and conifer needles—lying on the forest floor that can be readily set alight. A second factor is an increase in the number of forest fires started by humans, whether accidental or deliberate.

Many conifer forests are well adapted to fires (see "Fire in the taiga," pages 97–100). Some tree species, such as the jack pine and lodgepole pine, are specifically adapted to benefit from fires. Nevertheless, if intense, widespread forest fires break out too regularly, many tree species are killed off because they do not have enough time to mature and set seeds between one fire event and the next. This applies even to fire-adapted pine trees. Fires that occur too frequently reduce the diversity of tree life on which the forest community depends and favor fast-growing, opportunistic weeds. For most foresters, "weeds" are fast-growing herbaceous plants or shrubs that take up nutrients and shade the ground and thus prevent or delay saplings' establishment.

## Introductions of exotic species

Some taiga plants and animals have suffered losses because people have purposely introduced foreign species for commercial reasons. In Europe, for example, Sitka spruce is a fast-growing tree favored by timber merchants, who plant it in place of the naturally occurring but slower-growing Scotch pines. Among favored fur-bearing animals, North American mink were released into western Siberia in the 1920s and 1930s, and their success in the wild has impeded the recovery of wild sable populations with which they compete. Raccoon dogs, a member of the dog family native to southeastern Siberia, were released into European Russia from the mid-1920s in the hope of boosting wild fur production. The species flourished, and its range extended westward, reaching

Sweden by 1945. There, the species has become a nuisance, feeding on small game birds and mammals. The fur is also unusable, lacking the desirable long hairs sought by the fur industry and found in animals living to the east in the colder climates of Russia.

Of greater concern are invasive alien species that are introduced unintentionally. More than 200 nonnative (exotic) species are known to attack the trees in the taiga forests of North America. Most of these pests are insects that have been imported by accident in containers and packages of forestry or agricultural produce. In the 19th century, white pine blister rust, a parasitic fungus, was introduced into Canada in pine products imported from Europe. Today the rust damages white pines in much of Canada. In the border area between Canada and Washington State, the rust is responsible for devastating local populations of whitebark pine, with up to 90 percent mortality in some stands.

There are four major stages in the process of countering invasions by alien species: prevention, early detection, eradication, and, failing eradication, control. Once alien species are established, the eradication or control options are usually expensive and difficult to apply; prevention is usually the cheapest and most effective option. Prevention relies upon enforcing international regulations on the import of potentially contaminated material, intercepting and inspecting cargoes, and treating or disposing of suspect material. The World Conservation Union (IUCN) has developed a global strategy for the prevention and management of invasive alien species, and it is seeking to implement the strategy across the world through international conventions. Boreal forests are particularly vulnerable to damage by invasive insect or pathogenic (disease-causing) species because many forest stands have a low diversity of tree species.

## Hydroelectricity

Large-scale hydroelectric schemes, while apparently providing relatively clean energy at low cost, have negative environmental impacts. Dams cause changes to the valleys both upstream and downstream of the barrier. The dam holds back not only water but also silt. Downstream of the dam, the loss of silt tends to cause greater erosion of the riverbank. Upstream of the dam, the water that is held back creates a reservoir that floods a wide expanse of existing landscape. Immersed land plants die, and the subsequent decay of flooded woodland releases carbon dioxide and methane—both of which are major greenhouse gases. Historically, this effect has been left out of the cost-benefit analysis of dam-building.

Also of great importance are the social impacts of dams. People are displaced from the area where the reservoir forms. Because hydroelectric plants are often sited in wilderness areas, native peoples that lead a subsistence existence are often the ones displaced. Finally, dam creation changes the economic structure for people living in the wilderness region. New jobs—many of them temporary ones during the construction phase of the project—replace old sources of income. Those people who once lived a self-reliant subsistence existence now take jobs that are based on a money-based and market-driven economy. This radically changes their way of life, and people that once had a vested socioeconomic interest in maintaining the rich ecological diversity of the taiga may now no longer do so.

Between 1975 and 1990, around the southern end of Hudson Bay, Cree and other native peoples lost about 6,000 square miles (15,500 km$^2$) of land to dams and reservoirs. These hydropower systems were set up to provide power for Quebec and Ontario. They overturned the lives of taiga people living hundreds of miles from the final destination of the electricity. More recent plans to develop the wilderness of the Canadian shield have come under much stricter control.

In September 1993, Hydro-Québec, the state corporation responsible for Quebec's electricity supply, released a 5,000-page document outlining their plan to build three dams on the Great Whale River in a relatively unspoiled region near Hudson Bay. The plan was to build hydroelectric plants to meet Quebec's growing demand for electricity and to provide a surplus that could be exported to the United States. Environmental groups in Canada and the United States objected to the proposals on various grounds. They believed the project would push the river's sturgeon to extinction and that flooded vegetation decomposing in the dams' reservoirs would release mercury that would contaminate the reservoir water, making fish caught in it unsafe for human consumption. Representatives of the Cree community objected on the grounds that the dams would flood 5 percent of their territory—and an area particularly rich in game. They argued that the hydroelectric project would constitute an invasion of their land, overturning their local economy and way of life. The Cree representatives and environmental pressure groups eventually won the argument. In November 1994, the Quebec government canceled the Great Whale Project.

## Air pollution

Pollution is defined as alteration of specific physical or chemical factors in the environment, not ordinarily present at such levels, to the extent that they may cause harm to living organisms. Pollutants are those substances or factors that enter the environment at levels believed to be harmful. In practice, to demonstrate that a given chemical produces a specific effect on organisms in the environment is difficult and costly. Typically, the danger posed by a chemical is calculated based on laboratory studies in which organisms, or cultured tissues from organisms, are exposed to the chemical in question to see its effect. From such studies, scientists estimate acceptable levels of such chemicals in the environment. They err on the side of caution, usually setting the acceptable levels quite low. But the complexity of interactions in the environment makes such simple estimates difficult to translate to the real-world situation. Some organisms concentrate chemicals in certain tissues in their body, so the toxic effect of the pollutant is multiplied. Also, the environment contains a rich cocktail of chemicals that may interact with one another, so the combined effect of two different substances may be much worse than one chemical on its own. In classic studies carried out in the 1960s and reported in 1970, researchers studied the interaction of elevated levels of the gaseous pollutants sulfur dioxide ($SO_2$) and ozone ($O_3$) on eastern white pine trees in the Ohio River valley. The two gases, acting together, had a much greater damaging affect on trees than either on their own. Together, the pollutants caused poor needle growth, premature needle fall, and stunted tree growth overall.

The most widespread pollutants in the taiga are those that travel through the air. Most notable are oxides of sulfur and nitrogen, and ozone. Natural processes, such as volcanic action, release nitrogen and sulfur oxides. But more originate from human activities, especially the burning of fossil fuels such as coal, petroleum oils, and natural gas, and the heating of metals that contain sulfur impurities. Ozone forms in the lower atmosphere, the troposphere (see "Weather, climate, and atmosphere," pages 36–39), when nitrogen dioxide ($NO_2$) and certain hydrocarbons such as alkenes (included in the category of volatile organic compounds, or VOCs), are chemically altered by exposure to sunlight, a photochemical reaction. Both such ozone precursors are common products released from the burning of fossil fuels and are found in vehicle exhaust fumes at polluting levels.

Air pollution is not new. Medieval cities suffered from choking, smoke-rich air polluted by the burning of sulfur-rich coals for heating buildings, for cooking, and for many manufacturing processes, ranging from smelting metals to preserving foods by smoking them. In the late 1200s, Edward I of England enacted a law to stop people burning smoky coals in London. Nevertheless, by 1700, most English cities were scarred by oxides of sulfur and nitrogen oxides. The chemicals dissolved in moisture in the air to fall as acid rain. The rain etches into buildings, weakens clothes, and damages the leaves on trees.

With the industrial revolution of the 18th and 19th centuries, the burning of fossil fuels increased and air quality worsened. It was not until comparatively recently that governments have begun to take air pollution seriously and taken active steps to reduce it. In the United Kingdom, for example, the government passed the Clean Air Act in 1956, which established smokeless zones where only smoke-free fuels could be burned. This legislation was brought in after the dreadful winter of 1952, when thousands of Londoners died of respiratory diseases made worse by a sulfurous smog (a fog containing soot particles and sulfur dioxide) that choked the city.

While dealing with the most visible form of air pollution—namely, soot particles that produce a thick smog—the Clean Air Act initially did little to deal with the problem of oxides of sulfur and nitrogen. In fact, as industrialists built taller chimneys to reduce the fallout of atmospheric pollution locally, the problem shifted farther from its place of origin. Air pollution drifted hundreds of miles on air currents to affect neighboring countries. The smokestacks and car exhausts of British and German cities affect the lakes and forests of Scandinavia's taiga. Air pollution released in Chicago and Detroit falls as acid rain by the time it reaches Ontario, Quebec, Labrador, and Newfoundland.

Large expanses of the taiga are particularly susceptible to acid rain. Many taiga lakes and forests form above granite bedrock on the ancient rocky heartland—the so-called shield areas—of Canada, Scandinavia, and Russia. The soils here contain very little limestone, and the lakes hold little calcium carbonate. This is significant because these compounds can neutralize acid rain. In their absence, shield lakes and soils can become acidic quickly. Hundreds of shield lakes in Ontario have become so acidic (pH 4.5 or less) that they are now devoid of most animal life. How long they will take to recover is not known. Hundreds more lakes in Quebec, Canada, and in Sweden have pHs of 5–4.5 and are dangerously close to losing their fish populations and most of their invertebrates.

Acid rain became an internationally recognized problem in the 1970s. In June 1972, at the UN Conference on the Human Environment in Stockholm, Sweden, Swedish scientists claimed that acid gases released from countries in northwest Europe were drifting over Sweden and damaging lakes and forests. This claim triggered 20 years of research by European scientists that showed the Swedish scientists were largely correct but that the effects of acid rain were more complex than expected. The results prompted European governments to meet and establish international laws to combat air pollution that crosses international boundaries. It is not effective to treat the effects of acid-rain damage at their final destination. It has to be managed by reducing the release of the gases at their source.

Now many power stations and metal-smelting facilities incorporate devices for removing sulfur and nitrogen oxides from the fumes they release. Coal can be processed to remove much of its sulfur content before it is burned. Many cars now have combustion-efficient engines and run on low-sulfur fuels that produce lower levels of sulfur oxides in exhaust fumes. Such actions have resulted in a 50 percent reduction in European releases of sulfur gases between 1980 and 1999 and a slight lowering of levels of nitrogen oxide release. In the late 1990s, the United States and Canada combined were still releasing about 35 million U.S. tons (nearly 32 million tonnes) of sulfur dioxide into the atmosphere each year. These two countries have now agreed to reduce their sulfur dioxide emissions by one-third by 2010.

Acid rain is better called *acid deposition* because it is not just rain that causes the problem. Acid can travel through the air in snow, mist, fog, and even dry air. The damage acid deposition can cause is varied and sometimes quite indirect.

High levels of acid deposition can turn lake water quite acidic (pH less than 5), with the result that plants, invertebrates, and fish are killed or their reproduction affected. The

## Acidity and acid rain

Acidity is a measure of the concentration of hydrogen ions ($H^+$) in water. It is measured on a pH scale that ranges from 1 (most acidic) to 14 (most alkaline), with 7 being neutral. A solution (substances dissolved in a solvent, in this case water) with a pH of 6 is 10 times more acidic than a neutral solution; a pH 5 solution is 100 times more acidic. Most rainwater is slightly acidic (about pH 5.5) because of the dissolved carbon dioxide it contains, which forms carbonic acid. So-called acid rain has a pH of less than 5. The high acidity is caused by oxides of sulfur and nitrogen oxides that dissolve in water to form sulfuric, nitric, and other acids. Instances of highly acid rain, with a pH of less than 2.5, were reported in Europe and North America in the 1970s and 1980s. Such rainfalls are at least 1,000 times more acidic than typical rainwater.

highly acid water causes metals to dissolve out of the underlying ground, and some of these metals, such as mercury and aluminum, are toxic to people as well as other living organisms.

Acid deposition stresses trees, weakening them and making them more liable to other problems, such as attacks by insect pests or damage caused by extremes of weather. The soils in taiga forests are already acidic (with pHs below 5) because of the release of humic acids from slowly decomposing conifer needles. Greater acidity causes nutrients to leach down through the soil, away from shallow tree roots. At the same time, high acidity causes toxic aluminum to be released. Such loss of nutrients and release of metals weakens trees.

Acids can directly damage the waxy covering on conifer needles, causing water and nutrient loss that stunts tree growth. In Europe, severe acid deposition causes Norway spruce to shed its needles starting from the top of the tree. In North America, red spruce and sugar maple experience similar damage. Reductions in sulfur emissions in both North America and Europe have begun to halt the decline in the health of forest populations. In Europe, German and Scandinavian forests—among those worst affected by acid deposition—are showing signs of improvement. In North America, the damaged forests of eastern Canada and the northeastern United States have begun to show similar signs of improvement (see "Mapping a forest," pages 164–169). However, another phenomenon is coming to the fore. Ozone ($O_3$) levels in the troposphere are increasing worldwide, particularly downwind of major cities. Tropospheric ozone is not like the "good ozone" found in the stratosphere (see "Weather, climate, and atmosphere," pages 36–39) that is formed as a result of oxygen blocking some of the ultraviolet light that would otherwise reach Earth's surface. Tropospheric ozone is "bad ozone" in that at elevated levels it attacks the leaves of trees, damaging cells and lowering rates of photosynthesis, reducing leaf size, and causing premature leaf fall. Ozone is also implicated in weakening trees so that they are more likely to succumb to insect attack or fungal diseases.

In the 1970s and 1980s, studies of the eastern white pine in the United States showed that high levels of ground-level ozone reduced tree growth, increased rates of mortality, and decreased rates of reproduction. Some trees are genetically predisposed to be much more sensitive to ozone than others, and these trees are the first to succumb to damage. Tropospheric ozone is also a greenhouse gas estimated to contribute about 20 percent of the enhanced greenhouse effect (see the sidebar "The greenhouse effect," page 57).

While legislation to curb the release of sulfur oxides is well advanced in North America and Europe, the control of released nitrogen oxide and volatile organic compounds (VOCs) that produce ozone lags behind. These substances can produce ozone by photochemical reactions at locations thousands of miles from their point of origin, so that chemical releases in North America, for example, affect ozone levels in northwest Europe. For the current decade at least, tropospheric ozone is likely to be a significant issue affecting taiga forest in eastern Canada, the United States, and in northwest Europe. As China and former Soviet countries in central Europe and Asia industrialize, the ozone problem is likely to increase rather than decrease for Siberian and Far East Asian taiga in the foreseeable future.

## Mining, oil and gas, and pulp and paper industries

Mining activities and the wood pulp and paper industries are infamous sources of water pollution in the taiga. Extraction of natural gas and petroleum oil in Siberia, Canada, and Alaska has also resulted in major incidents of pollution during the 20th century.

In western Siberia between the mid-1960s and the 1980s, several oil and gas fields were exploited with little if any regard for potential environmental damage and no attempt to clean up drilling sites when they fell into disuse. As a result, tens of millions of acres of taiga forest, lakes, and rivers became contaminated by a cocktail of chemicals, including a variety of petroleum oils. In western Siberia, more than 40 million acres (16 million ha) of land previously suitable for hunting or reindeer grazing were lost. More than 60 rivers and dozens of major lakes and wetland areas were spoiled. Over the years, fires from natural gas wells burned down several million acres of forest.

Since the collapse of the USSR in 1991, the economic upheaval in Russia has meant that environmental concerns have taken a backseat. Russia has a fairly comprehensive set of environmental laws, but national and regional governments do not have the money or political will to enforce them. Cleaning up existing environmental problems is a low priority. For example, forested areas near Russia's nuclear weapon complexes at Chelyabinsk, Krasnoyarsk, and Tomsk are contaminated with radioactive material that is a hazard to people and wildlife. Lack of financial investment means that out-of-date, highly polluting factory machinery is kept in use without sufficient maintenance, rather than being replaced. New factories are built that breach environmental regulations, but such problems are overlooked because the new developments bring in vital jobs and income. In the current climate of economic instability, it is likely that many areas of Russia's south-central and southeastern taiga will be sold off to logging interests to raise cash in the short term rather than being protected in sustainable ways for the long term. Russian forestry experts estimate that Siberian forest production lost to diseases, pests, and fires in the 1990s was probably twice that of the 1980s (the lack of consistent methods of monitoring precludes a more definite statement).

The wood pulp and paper industry is a significant producer of water and air pollution in the taiga. Pulp and paper mills tend to be sited away from large towns and in heavily forested regions close to the source of wood. Pulping and papermaking processes require large volumes of water, so mills are typically located alongside rivers or large lakes.

Early stages in the preparation of wood pulp typically involve boats towing logs from close to where they are felled to processing mills. The floating logs block sunlight and so reduce levels of photosynthesis by freshwater plants. The lowering of plant productivity (the amount of plant tissue produced per unit area in a given time) means that less energy is passed on to river animals through the food web (see "Energy flow, food chains, and food webs," pages 91–95). In addition, wood fragments breaking off the logs fall to the riverbed and rot. The decay process, in which microbes extract some of the water's oxygen for their respiration, lowers levels of oxygen available to aquatic animals. The combination of lowered plant productivity and higher levels of microbial decomposition serves to lower the abundance and diversity of river fauna (animal life).

At their destination, the logs are taken out of the water and cut into shorter lengths. The bark is removed, and the short logs are cut, ground, or broken into chips. Sawdust and wood fragments that find their way into the river further block sunlight, reduce photosynthesis, and take up oxygen as they decay. The fragments also smother small organisms living on the riverbed.

The pulping process itself involves digesting wood chips to remove natural chemicals that cement wood fibers together. This involves several stages of washing, heating, and treating with strong alkalis (hydroxide chemicals that dissolve in water to produce highly alkaline solutions). A remarkably large amount of water is used in the process—typically well over 10,000 gallons of water for every U.S. ton of wood pulp. The wastewater contains various kinds of floating objects and dissolved substances that are potentially harmful to aquatic life. Pulp mills discharge water that contains natural organic substances washed out of the wood, such as lignin, terpenes, and phenols. They add to the load of organic substances that river organisms have to process. In addition, most phenols are toxic. Apart from the aquatic pollution, various sulfur compounds, including sulfur oxides are commonly released into the air from pulp mills. These can contribute to local acid rain and, together with released ammonia, give pulp mills their characteristic pungent smell.

Paper mills take wood pulp and compress it, with various binding and glossing agents, to produce paper. Increasingly, for economic and environmental reasons, paper mills recycle the chemicals they use. However, some pulp and paper mills use large quantities of chlorine to bleach pulp or paper to a bright white. Some chlorine or substances based on chlorine find their way into the environment either as gas or dissolved in water. Some chlorine-based organic substances—notably dioxins—are extremely toxic. In Canada, regional and federal laws limit the release of chlorine and chlorine-based substances into the environment. These tight regulations do not exist in Russia—or, where they do, they may not be policed. Some of the older pulp and paper mills still release a wide range of harmful substances into the air and have spectacularly polluted some of Siberia's rivers. In the 1990s, cellulose-processing factories on the banks of the Amur River in eastern Siberia were discharging sufficient polluted water to kill all the fish fry (newly hatched fish) for more than a mile downstream of each plant. Some of the Amur's tributaries were also receiving pollution from several metal works. The combined effect of these plants raised concentrations of zinc and copper in the river water and sediment to more than 100 times locally permitted levels. It is likely to be some years before the control of air, soil, and water pollution in the former USSR reaches similar levels to that found today in North American and northwest European countries.

## Climate change

The Earth's surface appears to be warming. In the last 100 years, the Earth's surface temperature has risen by about 1°F (0.6°C) overall. In 2001, the Intergovernmental Panel on Climate Change (IPCC) estimated that the global surface temperature will probably rise by between 2.5 and 10.4°F (1.4 and 5.8°C) between 1990 and 2100. Warming of some 9°F (5°C) since the last great ice age, some 15,000 years ago, was sufficient to transform the entire landscape of Canada from a wilderness deeply covered in snow and ice to the rich mixture of landscapes we see today. The predicted changes in our climate in the current century are cause for concern.

The Intergovernmental Panel on Climate Change's best guess for the global temperature rise between 1990 and 2100 is close to 5.4°F (3°C). However, because of natural cyclical effects and changes to the trade winds, northern latitudes where taiga is found are likely to warm more than this, particularly in the cold season. The implications for the taiga are worrisome.

Alaska is getting noticeably warmer and wetter. Between the early 1960s and the late 1990s, Alaska's average temperature across the seasons rose by about 5°F (3°C). Over a similar period, annual precipitation increased roughly 30 percent, with most of this increase occurring in central and northern Alaska. Other taiga regions are becoming drier. In northern Ontario, researchers in the Experimental Lakes Area noticed that evaporation from the lakes and forests in the snow-free season increased by about 30 percent over the decade of the 1990s.

Warmer, drier conditions could trigger surprisingly rapid changes in taiga forest. In southern Alaska, the 1990s saw more than 2 million acres (800,000 ha) of mature spruce forest succumbing to the ravages of the spruce bark beetle. Scientists suspect that two main effects caused the explosive increase in numbers of this insect pest. Both are linked to climate change. First, the trees are being weakened by lack of water due to a drier climate. Second, the milder winters are favoring the beetle's survival over winter.

Climate change will probably alter the nature of biological communities in taiga lakes and rivers too. As inland waters warm, species from the south are likely to invade fresh waters currently located in taiga regions, altering the balance of species in their communities. Present freshwater species of the taiga—cold-water fish such as lake trout, grayling, and dolly varden—could be replaced by warmer-water species, such as pike and walleye. Meanwhile, some freshwater taiga species could be displaced northward into what is now tundra territory. In addition, climatologists suspect that thousands of boreal forest lakes and wetlands might dry up in the next 100 years as levels of precipitation fall. While shifts in Earth's climatic regime occur regularly, at different scales of magnitude and at time scales ranging from decades to thousands of years, the current concern is that human-induced climate change is producing a massive climate shift within a century. This short period of time may be too abrupt for species to disperse successfully from their existing distributions to new ones. Without further human intervention, such as people helping to facilitate the transfer of species to new locations, many populations could be wiped out and the survival of taiga species threatened.

Climate change is also affecting the permafrost. Again, the concern is not so much that this is happening, but the speed with which it is doing so, so threatening the existing biological communities that have adapted to its presence. Since the 1980s, researchers at the University of Alaska have been recording loss of permafrost, particularly discontinuous permafrost (areas where the permafrost is patchy). Communities in Alaska and northern Canada are changing their construction practices. New schools and medical facilities are being built on solid, higher ground to avoid the lower-lying permafrost areas where permafrost may melt and become unstable. Most atmospheric scientists agree that a substantial proportion of the global temperature rise over the last century—at least half—can be accounted for by a rise in atmospheric levels of greenhouse gases produced by human activities. The obvious way to halt global warming is for governments to work together to cut down the release of greenhouse gases. This means reducing the amount of fossil fuels being burned. The Kyoto Protocol, an international agreement on reducing greenhouse gas emissions negotiated in 1997, seeks to lower greenhouse gas release by about 5 percent before 2012. Canada has ratified the treaty and hopes to make the cuts by offering incentives to people to make their homes more energy efficient. The Canadian government is also encouraging the use of cleaner gasoline and biodiesel, made from vegetable oil, as fuels that burn to produce fewer oxides of nitrogen (some forms of which are greenhouse gases). As of March 2005, the United States had declined to sign the protocol although Russia, following the example set by more than 140 countries, had recently done so.

# CONCLUSION: MANAGING THE TAIGA

Forests cover more than 60 percent of the taiga; the remainder consists of lakes, rivers, and wetlands such as peat bogs (these habitats are considered in other volumes in the series). Forest management is the application of scientific, economic, and social principles to the use of forests. Since the 1950s, there has been a gradual shift in attitudes among forest managers operating in boreal forests. Prior to this, they usually considered sustainable management of forests to be focused on sustainable timber production. Today, international agencies such as the Food and Agriculture Organization (FAO) of the United Nations encourage an "ecosystem approach" to sustainable management. This means managing forested lands in a way that maintains their biodiversity, productivity, and regenerative capacity in order to fulfill a range of biological, economic, and social functions, while limiting damage to other ecosystems. The table on page 166 shows some of the products and services a region of boreal forest can provide.

## Mapping a forest

The first consideration in managing a forest is estimating the extent and composition of the resource to be managed. Part of this process is to map the distribution of different types of biological community within the taiga forest. As we have seen, taiga forests support rich communities of plants, animals, and microbes. The nature of these communities varies with local climate, the nature of the soil, and patterns of disturbance. It also changes over time due to such events as tree-felling by humans, outbreaks of fungal diseases and pest insects, or natural forest fires.

In the latter half of the 20th century, the use of remote-sensing cameras mounted on aircraft or satellites revolution-

## Forests and freshwater

Boreal forests are not separate from other biomes that surround them but exchange energy and nutrients with them. In particular, the quality and volume of water in streams, rivers, and lakes downstream of a forest are greatly influenced by the nature of the forest.

Conifer trees are particularly good at intercepting water that is flowing across the soil surface or percolating through the soil. Tree roots and the accompanying ground cover and leaf litter on the forest floor physically block the flow of water as well as absorbing water. The extensive network of roots and mycorrhizal fungi helps stabilize the soil. As a result, volumes of water runoff and levels of waterborne soil particles are much lower downstream of an intact, mature forest than they would be if the forest were partially cleared. Several North American studies of mixed-temperate and boreal forests have revealed that runoff gullies several feet deep often form on newly cleared land following heavy rainfall. Rates of runoff on heavily cleared land are many times greater than on forested land nearby, with each acre of cleared land losing more than 10 U.S. tons of soil per acre (22 tonnes/ha) in a year—more than 10 times that of forested land nearby. In the 1990s, studies in northern Minnesota revealed that when 70 percent of the forest cover on a small watershed was clear-cut, small to medium-size floods increased in frequency, although the larger, less frequent floods (occurring at less than 30-year intervals) were probably unaffected.

Well-managed forests improve water quality in streams and rivers fed by the watershed. They accomplish this by cycling nutrients such as nitrates and phosphates, holding back sediment, and retaining some heavy metals. People living outside the boreal forest biome who use water drawn from it receive these benefits for free—but they may not know it. If they were made more aware of these ecological services and how much it would cost to replace them, it is likely they would support steps to preserve healthy forests in nearby taiga watersheds. Ideally, financial incentives provided by regional or national governments, or by water utilities, could contribute financially to the maintenance of well-managed forests in taiga watersheds.

ized the ability to map dense forest. Investigators can often assess the nature of the forest from images showing the color of tree foliage and the shape of trees as seen from the air. This information is coupled with geological knowledge about the nature of the soil and the shape of the land (topography). Taken together, this information allows scientists to predict

## Some boreal-forest products and services

| | |
|---|---|
| **Non-wood products** | Plants as sources of herbs and pharmaceuticals |
| | Leaves, seeds, berries, lichens, and fungi as food for livestock and people |
| | Animals such as reindeer and freshwater fish as human food |
| **Ecosystem services** | Regulation of climate and atmospheric composition at different scales of magnitude, ranging from local to regional to global |
| | Reduction of soil erosion by wind and water |
| | Slope stabilization |
| | Freshwater purification |
| | Nutrient and water storage |
| **Social and recreational services** | Living space for people |
| | Location for a wide range of outdoor recreational activities, including walking, skiing, bird-watching, landscape painting, and hunting |

the kinds of forest that are likely to grow in a given location even if the tree cover has not been surveyed directly at ground level. In many places, foresters carry out ground surveys of the trees growing in their locality and report their findings back to regional and federal agencies. In Canada, for example, the Canadian Forest Service in conjunction with Natural Resources Canada, the federal department mandated to promote the sustainable development and use of natural resources, compiles such data to produce maps and charts. The maps and charts show the distribution of forest types and the degree to which they are affected by human activities.

Roads are obvious features visible from the air. The number of roads in a given area is a sign of the level of fragmentation of a forested region. The more roads, the greater the fragmentation. People follow roads. In Canada and Russia, the development of road networks is usually a good indication that further disruptive development will follow shortly (see "Fragmentation," pages 148–149).

From 1993 to 1997, a NASA-sponsored examination of Canadian taiga called Boreal Ecosystem–Atmosphere Study (BOREAS) used satellite images recording different wavelengths of light to identify not only different species but also different stages in their growth. Studies such as BOREAS are revealing that the boreal landscape is more complex than previously thought. Rather than vast expanses of near-identical forest, the taiga forest forms a patchwork or mosaic that varies in the balance of species and age of dominant trees from locality to locality. Fires, insect attacks, and tree-felling are key factors that affect the age and species composition of areas that establish themselves according to climate, soil type, and topography.

Mapping tree distribution is one thing, but what about the health of these trees? The condition of forest trees can be assessed fairly quickly using various measures. For conifers, the loss of needles from the crown of the plant and "dieback" from the ends of branches are commonly used as an indicator of tree health. Crown-needle loss and branch dieback suggest ill health due to air pollution or other stresses to the tree, such as poor soil quality, attack by insect pests, or fungal diseases. In broad-leaved trees, similar stress indicators are used together with measures of leaf transparency in the crown of the plant. Transparency is a measure of the amount of light that passes through a leaf. In sugar maple, healthy leaves near the crown have a transparency of less than 25 percent; in other words, less than one-quarter of the available light passes through the leaves. If more than 35 percent of light passes through crown leaves, the plant is regarded as stressed. In the late 1980s and early 1990s, levels of transparency and dieback fell among sugar maples in eastern Canada, suggesting that levels of atmospheric sulfur dioxide pollution were declining (see "Air pollution," pages 153–158). Such information helps scientists put forward a strong case for the benefits of managing air pollution to maintain or improve forest health.

Knowing the age structure of the forest—the proportions of trees of different ages—also helps managers evaluate forest health and productivity. For example, a forest region that contains dominant trees of the same species and same age may be one that is being exploited intensively for its wood supplies. Alternatively, it could have suffered recent fire damage or a devastating insect pest attack. Whatever the cause, many trees have been removed and replaced by trees that established themselves at the same time. If human harvesting is the major factor accounting for this age structure, then

*Statistics for Canada's managed forests (Courtesy of Natural Resources Canada, 2000)*

| forest harvesting | | | |
|---|---|---|---|
| | area | acres | hectares |
| | clear-cut | 2,283,669 | 924,188 |
| | selectively cut | 255,805 | 103,523 |
| | **total** | **2,539,474** | **1,027,711** |

| forest regeneration | | | |
|---|---|---|---|
| | area | acres | hectares |
| | seedlings | 1,515,183 | 613,186 |
| | seeded | 46,727 | 18,910 |
| | **total** | **1,561,910** | **632,096** |

such uniform forests probably support relatively low biodiversity. A similar forest could be managed to contain a narrow range of dominant tree species, but of a wide variety of ages, by clear-cutting moderately small areas in a rotation at prescribed time intervals. Such a forest would contain a patchwork of habitats at various stages in succession, which means that it might support a wide variety of habitats and, in turn, a wider variety of wildlife.

Human activities have had a major impact on the extent and health of boreal forests. But how much effect? One way to find out is to compare present-day taiga forests with those that existed before human interference. In Canada, for example, researchers examine historical records and early surveys to see where forests existed in historical times. They examine the remains of tree pollen in peat bogs and lake sediments. This extends the record for which trees lived further back in time. To complete the picture, scientists use existing knowledge of the climate and soil preferences of today's trees and work out where such trees might have grown in historic or prehistoric times when climates were different from those today.

Another approach to assessing human impact on forest health is to protect areas of forest from human activity and to

## The age of Canada's trees

Much of Canada's forest is made up of stands or large patches of trees of similar age. They have become established following major disturbance, such as fire, insect attack, or harvesting. Most of the oldest forest lies in the Pacific Maritime region of British Columbia. Here major fires and outbreaks of insect pests are rare, and hemlock, cedar, and fir trees typically live for several hundred years. In the boreal forests of Alberta, Saskatchewan, and Manitoba, about one-third to one-half of the trees are more than 120 years old. In the eastern forests of Ontario, Quebec, and Labrador, one-tenth or less of the trees reach 120 years old. This is partly because these forests contain species that are naturally short-lived, such as trembling aspen and balsam fir. It is also because of higher levels of harvesting and regular disturbance from forest fires and/or insect attacks.

compare what happens in protected areas with what is happening in unprotected ones (see "Protected areas," pages 181–183). The protected areas also provide a stronghold for rare and endangered species. However, protected areas are affected by human factors beyond their boundaries. Atmospheric pollution and land-use changes outside protected areas alter the climate and water availability within protected areas.

One way to monitor ongoing changes in the health and vitality of a forest community is to consider biodiversity (biological diversity).

## Biodiversity

Biodiversity, or biological diversity, is a measure of the variety of life. Biologists measure biodiversity at different levels of organization, such as the amount of genetic variation in a species (genetic diversity), the range of species or groups of species within a locality (species diversity), and the diversity of ecosystems within an area (ecosystem diversity).

Biologists and environmentalists regard loss of biodiversity as important for several reasons. Biodiversity is important in maintaining ecosystem functions. For example, mixed forest vegetation reduces flooding and soil erosion. Where sloping land is clear-cut, the absence of a rich mixture of vegetation types results in rainfall running off the land rather than being retained. By retaining water, the vegetation above, on, and below the ground—in concert with microbes—performs functions such as water storage and water purification (see the sidebar "Forests and freshwater," page 165). Through photosynthesis, taiga ecosystems also replenish the oxygen in air and reduce its carbon dioxide load. The diverse community of organisms works together to perform ecosystem functions, and we do not understand enough about how ecosystems work to know which organisms are most important to the health of the community. We may be overlooking microscopic organisms that play vital roles.

Moreover, there is a strong utilitarian argument not to destroy life-forms because they may have properties that might be useful to us in the future. Many taiga plants produce chemicals that have useful medical properties. Many

*A hint at the wildlife experience to be found at Wonder Lake in Denali National Park, Alaska. Mount Denali lies in the background. (Courtesy of Michio Hoshino/ Minden Pictures)*

more substances might be out there, lurking in microbes beneath the soil. We may never discover some of them if, for example, we destroy the rare orchid plants that are symbiotic partners of some of these microbes.

Finally, some argue for the moral and aesthetic merits of preserving taiga. The moral argument is that we do not have the right to damage habitats and endanger species simply to make money. A more person-centered view is that by removing life-forms and the beautiful places where they live, we are denying our children and grandchildren the opportunity to see nature's masterpieces.

Based on studies of tropical rain forests carried out in the 1990s, researchers have found that the diversity of life-forms and their living environments typically decrease along the spectrum of land-use types, from old-growth forest to regenerated forest, plantation forest, and agricultural land. Such a pattern is generally assumed to hold for boreal forests, although the studies to back this claim have yet to be completed. However, study of the *ecological niche,* the role a species plays within an ecosystem, does make it possible to assess the likelihood that species will disappear if environmental conditions change. In northern Finland, for example, a variety of well-studied species—including orchids, the capercaillie, the Siberian tit, and martens—depend on habitats found in old-growth forest. Their numbers decline dramatically where stands of mixed-species, mixed-age conifers are gradually replaced by single-species, single-age stands managed intensively for their wood. At the same time, much of the diversity among insect and fungal communities is lost, although less is known about the ecological niches of these smaller organisms.

One way to track biodiversity at the species and ecosystem levels is to monitor species or groups of species and see whether their populations change in density or geographic distribution over many years. Such changes can be correlated with shifts in land use and other environmental impacts, such as pollution. Done properly, this would involve experts in a wide range of specialties gathering samples from the study area, identifying the species, and recording the numbers of individuals of each, their size distribution, and their biomass. This process would need to be repeated at intervals of decades. Such studies are expensive and time consuming, however, and at present, there is a shortage of experts who can identify small organisms to species level. As a result, biodiversity studies tend to be much narrower in scope. Typically only a few key indicator species are studied, and it is assumed that if these organisms are changing, so are many others. In the case of particular tree species on which many species, ranging from fungi and insects to rodents and deer of the boreal forest community depend, this is a reasonable assumption.

## Endangered species in Canada's taiga

The Committee on the Status of Endangered Wildlife in Canada (COSEWIC) classifies endangered species as those facing extinction within Canada within a matter of decades. Threatened species are those that could become endangered over a similar timescale. Vulnerable species are those that are especially sensitive to natural disturbances or certain human activities.

Parts of Canada's taiga harbor four large terrestrial vertebrate species that are classified as endangered: the spotted owl, cougar, wolverine, and Newfoundland pine marten. In Canada, wolverines and woodland caribou are the most widespread large taiga mammals that are classed as vulnerable or threatened across much of their range. Wolverines require mature or old-growth coniferous forests, and they suffer from even low levels of human disturbance. The removal of old-growth forests, high levels of hunting and trapping in the past, and increased human intrusion into wilderness areas have all taken their toll on wolverine numbers, particularly in eastern Canada.

The case of woodland caribou in British Columbia, Canada, hints at the complexity of relationships among forest species. In British Columbia's interior mountains, greater tree harvesting in the last few decades has produced large areas of regenerating forest populated by young trees. Moose favor saplings as food, and the moose population has gradually increased as more food has become available. The moose population, in turn, supports a larger population of wolves that feed upon these large deer. The wolves take caribou as well as moose, and so the caribou population has been affected and has declined. Only by closely monitoring the populations of the different species and their interactions did scientists reveal the underlying pattern. Armed with such information, biologists have strong arguments to influence the activities of foresters to help maintain a more biodiverse forest community.

Increasingly, Canada's field biologists are monitoring groups of species in certain localities to look for habitat alterations, population changes, and species interactions. At the top of their lists are breeding songbirds, moose and caribou, and scarce predatory mammals such as Newfoundland pine martens. In some localities, moose and caribou are keystone species; this means their loss is likely to have a major effect on many other local species. In Alberta, trained volunteers are encouraged to take part in bird-banding operations, in which people attach numbered bands to birds' legs to identify them in later surveys. Monitoring populations of banded birds enables biologists to follow bird migration patterns, track changes in population number, and identify key factors in bird conservation, such as locating critical habitats for successful nesting.

In Canada, although very few boreal forest species are threatened with extinction, many species occupy less than half the territory they occupied 200 years ago. This has come about because of habitat loss—in particular, the clearing of forests for agriculture and settlement. Harvesting of timber has removed the older trees on which a variety of animals and other plants depend, and hunting and trapping has added to the toll on specific larger mammals.

Today, some Canadian provinces are taking steps to halt the shrinking ranges of threatened tree species. In Newfoundland and Labrador, for example, the federal governments established the White Pine Advisory Group, which is taking steps to protect existing stands of white pine and plant new ones. Before this action, the trees had failed to recover from extensive harvesting of pine for shipbuilding in the late 1800s and early 1900s. In the 1990s, the group established an annual white-pine harvest at about one-quarter the volume harvested in 1900.

## Maintaining genetic diversity

Genetic diversity is vital if a species is to be able to evolve and adapt to change. Without genetic diversity, populations become inbred (see "Fragmentation," pages 148–149). If environmental conditions change to the detriment of the population, many of the individuals are likely to die, and the population is in danger of extinction. In conserving populations, therefore, it is also important to conserve their genetic diversity.

Canada's major commercial softwood species have high levels of genetic diversity. White and black spruce, jack pine, lodgepole pine, and balsam fir are all wind pollinated. They do not require animals to transfer the pollen from one tree to another, which could make them vulnerable should their pollinators become threatened. Many taiga trees benefit, however, when squirrels and birds disperse their seeds.

Nevertheless, some of the Canadian taiga's trees are genetically impoverished. The red pine, for example, appears to have experienced a "genetic bottleneck" in its evolutionary history—a period when the population was markedly reduced in size and had little genetic variation overall. This may help explain why the species is restricted to quite narrow environmental conditions—namely, sandy, well-drained soils where the vegetation is frequently burned back in ground fires. Western red cedar and red spruce also have low levels of genetic variation, and the impact of this on their vulnerability to harvesting is currently being researched.

In Canada, conservationists use a range of strategies to maintain or even enhance the genetic diversity of particular tree species. They can help ensure that foresters sow seeds that come from stocks that are adapted to local conditions. They can advise foresters to grow particular tree species, such as white pines, in sufficient densities so that they cross-pollinate (which maintains genetic variation) rather than self-pollinate (which is likely to diminish it).

Plant breeders can maintain high genetic diversity by selectively breeding a wide range of forms within a species. Plant breeders create strong hybrids by crossing plants from distinct strains with favorable qualities. Ideally, to maintain the genetic diversity of a commercial species, plant breeders should cultivate plantations of locally adapted strains across the geographical range of the species. Hybrids that are likely to flourish in particular environmental conditions can be bred by crossing suitable strains from different geographic locations.

Strains with particular features such as fast-growth capability and disease resistance can be cloned; this process mimics asexual reproduction by artificially creating many genetically identical individuals from the same source. *Tissue culture* is a modern approach to cloning. Clusters of cells from the growing parts of a seedling are separated and encouraged to grow in a sterile, carefully controlled environment in the laboratory. From these cell clusters, hundreds of genetically identical young plants can be grown and then transplanted to their final sites to grow to maturity. Some seedlings are retained to continue the tissue-cultured strain, generation after generation.

A step beyond tissue culture is *genetic engineering,* where individual genes are effectively "cut-and-pasted" using high-tech methods to create strains that would never occur in nature.

## The world's biggest clone?

Clones are individuals that are genetically identical to one another. In nature, clones usually arise by asexual reproduction (reproduction involving no mixing of genetic material). Trembling aspen, Canada's most widespread hardwood species, reproduces asexually by sending out suckers that sprout new roots and shoots, particularly after major disturbances such as fires or tree-felling. A clone of aspen trees can cover more than a hundred acres and contains many thousands of genetically identical mature stems all originating from a single parent. Aspens also reproduce sexually. Across Canada, there are many genetically distinct forms of aspen, each forming stands of naturally cloned trees adapted to local conditions.

Genes from entirely different species can be inserted into conifer trees to give them novel properties. Studies are currently under way to develop genetically engineered spruce trees that grow faster while requiring fewer nutrients than conventional strains. In time, strains can be developed with specific wood properties that enable the trees to be pulped more easily. Within a decade or two it is likely that genetic engineers will create conifers that can manufacture their own fungicides and insecticides.

## Tree harvesting

With forest managers gradually adopting ecosystem management principles, taiga forests are increasingly managed to meet a number of different needs. Not all can be sustained within a given stand, and decisions need to be made about priorities for a given stand of trees. In stands of single-species, high-value trees, well-managed clear-cutting may be the best option. In wildlife parks, where conservation and recreational values have a high priority, selective cutting may be more appropriate.

In clear-cutting, the removal of trees alters the forest microclimate (the climate near the ground), typically replacing damp, shady conditions with dry, sunlit ones. Tree removal also massively alters the input of organic (carbon-rich) substances to the soil. This is partly because the regular, annual input of forest litter is interrupted and partly because living trees, as mycorrhizal partners of soil fungi, are temporarily absent. Depending on how the clear-cut was managed, logging debris (slash) such as fallen leaves, broken branches, and tree stumps and their roots may litter the ground and provide organic matter for decomposers to return to the soil. But if trees do not rapidly reestablish, soil organisms deprived of fresh supplies of leaf litter may die out. So, too, might mycorrhizal fungi deprived of their living partner trees.

For reasons such as these, the shape and size of a clear-cut can be critical for successful forest regeneration. If a narrow strip of forest is clear-cut, rather than a square or circular patch, each part of the clear-cut area is relatively close to the existing forest that surrounds the patch. The strip will be largely ecotone, with the surrounding forest still providing shade, an input of seeds and nutrient-releasing plant matter, and a living network of mycorrhizal fungi extending into the patch. In most cases, clear-cut strips are much more likely to regenerate than square or circular clear-cut patches of the same area.

So, clear-cutting is not simply "bad." It depends on the particular environmental circumstances and the manner in which the clear-cutting is carried out. For example, clear-cutting can be an appropriate means of salvaging forests ravaged by insect infestations, either to limit the extent of such outbreaks or at least to salvage economically the fallen trees. In the 1980s and 1990s, clear-cutting of conifers in the Bowron River region of central British Columbia was prompted by the spread of spruce bark beetles into this area from nearby Wells Gray Provincial Park. While this clear-cutting is often quoted by environmentalists and the media as an overly aggressive harvesting policy, it was, perhaps, an appropriate response to limit the further spread of the outbreak and remove the reservoir of infested wood.

In Alaska, Canada, Scandinavia, and the former Soviet Union, some old-growth forests have become sphagnum bog forests because the cool soil has become overly damp, too acidic, and nutrient-poor in its surface layers through leaching. Periodic disturbance by insect infestations, fungal disease, or fire can prevent forest from reverting to boggy ground, and so could well-managed clear-cutting. In such situations, clear-cutting could reinvigorate the forest and prevent it from "deteriorating."

Clear-cutting may not be appropriate in the most northerly taiga regions. These are subjected to severe frosts in winter, and regrowth may not occur if all the tree cover is removed and little or no ground cover is left to retain surface warmth. In such circumstances, the permafrost could rise to the surface, preventing regrowth. Clear-cutting is likewise not appropriate where boreal forest is growing on steep, potentially unstable slopes, because tree removal there will markedly increase the risk of soil erosion, landslides, and snow avalanches. Where many small streams flow through a forest, clear-cutting anything other than small areas would probably alter runoff, local stream flows, and freshwater quality.

Finally, where the aesthetic features of the landscape have a particularly high premium, clear-cuts are probably not appropriate, or they need to be managed in such a way as to create minimal visual impact.

## Assisting forest regeneration

In Canada's boreal forest, as elsewhere in the taiga, clear-cutting is still the most common method for harvesting trees. This results in large patches of conifer forest containing trees of similar ages.

If a forest area is felled so that most of its larger trees are removed, then natural regeneration can replace the lost trees. In Canada in the early 2000s, natural regeneration was adopted to replace nearly half of the taiga forest that was felled annually. However, the trees that grow may not be of the same species as those removed, and it may take many decades before a secondary succession reestablishes forest that is similar to the original. For such reasons, foresters assist natural regenerative processes using artificial methods.

As we have seen earlier (see "Renewal and succession," pages 95–97) toxins in the decaying matter on the forest floor can prevent seeds from germinating. If trees are cut down, seeds may still not germinate even if they are present in the topsoil. It is becoming common practice for foresters to burn back the ground cover or scarify (loosen the soil surface) to help provide the right conditions for seeds to germinate.

If forest regeneration is likely to be slow—for instance, because there are no suitable trees nearby to provide seeds—then foresters may resort to planting seeds or seedlings. This way foresters can both control the species that reestablish and speed up the reforestation process. Foresters need to choose seeds or seedlings of the right genetic stock—plants that are adapted to the local conditions—if tree growth is to be successful. Artificially planting seeds or seedlings is expensive, but the effort is justified if the resulting tree growth is rapid and well controlled, yielding an economically worthwhile harvest of timber or pulp. Planting and seeding programs became common in Canada in the late 1980s because forest managers recognized that many cleared forest areas had failed to restock themselves quickly. By the mid-1990s, about 90 percent of harvested sites on crown lands (lands retained by Canada's federal government) were showing good signs of regeneration within 10 years. By the early 2000s, planting seedlings was used for regenerating forest in about half the acreage of forest cleared annually.

## Fire as a management tool

Intense forest fires that ravage a locality every few years can have catastrophic effects on the diversity of life in the forest (see "Fire in the taiga," pages 97–100). Nevertheless, since the 1960s, conservationists have come to understand that most forest fires are a natural part of the life cycle of the forest. Increasingly, firefighters control natural fires to avoid damage to human life and property while allowing some large fires in remote forests to burn almost uncontrolled. Firefighters can monitor the progress of a fire using land-based or aircraft-mounted infrared cameras. These devices reveal the intensity of the fire, and by monitoring relative temperatures of different patches of ground, firefighters can plot the progress of the fire even where flames are not clearly visible. Various fire-suppression methods, such as spraying water or fire-retarding chemicals or cutting or burning firebreaks, can help contain the spread of the fire.

Today controlled fires are used as a tool to help manage the growth of the forest. By setting small, controlled fires, foresters can burn away dead or dying vegetation. This clears the ground for new growth but also prevents the buildup of tinder that could be ignited by lightning, which could trigger much fiercer and more widespread fires.

Controlled burns need to be set with great care so they do not become uncontrolled. Experienced foresters choose conditions when the forest tinder is not too dry and the wind is moderately weak, steady, and blowing in the planned direction. Such conditions encourage a low flame that burns slowly across the forest floor.

Controlled fires can destroy ground-cover plants and prepare the soil for germination of conifer seeds by destroying toxins in the soil's surface layer. At the same time, the fire destroys insect pests and, through burning vegetation, recycles nutrients that are returned to the soil. Use of controlled fires as a management tool is still in its fairly early stages, but the method is likely to gain in importance as scientists come to better understand the benefits—and shortcomings—of controlled fire damage.

## Controlling forest pests

Fungal diseases and pest insects are two of the most significant agents of damage to taiga trees. Overall, fungal diseases account for about twice as much economic damage to conifer trees as insect pests. Diseases such as white pine blister rust and root rot can stunt the growth of pine trees and kill a proportion of mature trees, often by making them more susceptible to other disease agents. Bark beetles cause tree damage by boring through the bark and laying eggs in the soft tissue beneath that hatch to consume the inner bark that contains part of the tree's nutrient-transport system. An infestation by more than 1,000 grubs can disrupt the rings of living tissues within a tree trunk, killing the tree within a month.

In North America since the 1970s, increased criticism by environmental lobbies over the use of insecticides—insect-controlling chemicals—has resulted in their more limited use in recent years. In more remote locations, however, spraying insecticides from aircraft is still an effective means of controlling some spruce budworm and sawfly infestations. Today, many authorities favor the use of an integrated pest management (IPM) approach. This involves combining more than one pest-control strategy. Biological control agents—for instance, natural predators, parasites, or disease organisms of the pest insect such as the bacterium *Bacillus thuringiensis*—are encouraged or introduced. Reservoirs of the pest insect such as fallen, decayed trees are removed, where possible. And the creation of so-called *heterotypes* (mixed-age, mixed-species stands) rather than *monotypes* (large single-age, single-species stands) is encouraged. Foresters can adopt cropping and planting cycles that gradually convert monotypes to heterotypes.

Over millions of years, pest insects have become specialized to feed not only on a particular species of tree but also on a particular stage in the tree's life cycle. Spruce budworm kills older trees; white pine weevils attack the fast-growing tip of young trees. In a monoculture of trees of similar ages, an infested tree is surrounded by other plants of the same type and age ready for the pest insect to colonize and spread. In mixed-age, mixed-species stands, the pest insects have to travel farther to find a suitable tree to colonize, and the likelihood for the pest to be eaten or killed en route is greater.

## Protected areas

Protected forest areas provide refuges for species that are under threat elsewhere. They also offer ecological benchmarks for comparison with disturbed forest regions, as well as providing the recreational benefits of a wilderness experience.

Across the world's taiga, there are currently more than 1,000 protected areas recognized by the World Conservation Union (IUCN), the world's largest environmental conservation organization, with members from some 140 countries, including more than 100 government agencies and 750 non-governmental organizations (NGOs). The areas vary greatly in size and degree of protection, and many straddle adjacent biomes, such as tundra, mixed forest, and prairies (steppes). Some large protected areas form part of the United Nations Educational, Scientific and Cultural Organization (UNESCO) program on Man and the Biosphere (MAB). This program, launched in 1970 and growing annually, is dedicated to establishing protected areas for representative ecosystems. A special feature is its focus on gathering and communicating scientific knowledge on biodiversity conservation in tandem with fostering the sustainable development of local human communities.

Within the main belt of taiga lie more than 12 biosphere reserves. The U.S. state of Alaska contains the 6-million-acre (2.4-million-ha) Denali National Park, which incorporates

Mount McKinley, North America's tallest mountain. Canada has two much smaller taiga reserves—Riding Mountain in Manitoba and Charlevoix in Quebec—that conserve typical taiga species as well as rare ones. Riding Mountain, for example, contains the world's largest herd of wood bison (see the sidebar "Wood bison," page 86). The remaining biosphere reserves lie in Eurasia, with more than seven in the Russian Federation. The Central Siberian reserve (Tzentralnosibirskii) is the largest of all, encompassing 12 million acres (about 5 million ha).

Canada's Charlevoix reserve and Russia's Pechoro-Ilychskiy reserve, on the western flanks of the Urals, serve to illustrate some of the problems that beset protected taiga areas. The Charlevoix reserve, set up in the late 1980s, contains lowland and highland taiga as well as an important wetland region drained by the St. Lawrence River and its tributaries. The lowlands contain spruce, pine, fir, and maple forest through which lynx and caribou roam and beavers swim. Caribou, previously made locally extinct by hunting, were reintroduced in the 1960s.

Today, the reserve is a popular destination for wildlife tourism, with local scientists educating the public about the nature of the reserve and its inhabitants. Despite its secure protected status, threats to the reserve continue. The biggest threat to Charlevoix is pollution. At ground level, ozone pollution originating from southern Canada and the northeastern United States still poses a threat to the health of Charlevoix's forests. More than 2,000 companies empty pollutants into the St. Lawrence and its tributaries, raising levels of heavy metals and artificial chemicals such as polychlorinated biphenyls (PCBs). These have reached the point where they threaten the health of fish and aquatic mammals.

Russia's Pechoro-Ilychskiy reserve contains three main types of habitat: a lowland plain with open pine forests and sphagnum bogs; foothills covered with dark taiga (spruce and fir); and a mountainous region of alpine meadows, tundra, and birch forests. Access to the region is quite difficult, but historically the area has been popular with hunters. Among Pechoro-Ilychskiy's inhabitants are 500 species of taiga plants, 200 types of bird, 17 fish species, and 40 types of mammals, including brown bears, wolverines, sables, pine martens, red squirrels, and beavers. The reserve contains the world's first elk farm, and continuous study of these deer over 50 years has yielded important knowledge about elk behavior.

When the Pechoro-Ilychskiy reserve was set up in 1930, it was more than 50 percent larger than its present size. In the 1950s it shrank to 10 percent of its former size when economic difficulties caused the government to change the geographical boundaries. The reserve then grew to nearly its current size in 1959. Despite its protected status, between the 1950s and 1980s some of its forests were felled and elk and reindeer hunting began. In 1984, Pechoro-Ilychskiy was given international biosphere reserve status and greater protection. The biggest threat to the reserve is not pollution but changes in government policy—or a lack of political will or funding to enforce laws—so that the reserve is once again threatened with unregulated hunting, tree-felling, and other developments.

It is not possible to generalize on the success, or otherwise, of existing protected areas such as those in the UNESCO-MAB program. However, by giving protected areas special status and then studying them and fostering their development, the UNESCO-MAB program is seeking to find workable solutions to resource conservation issues. Meanwhile, forests face increasing pressures caused, not least, by human population growth.

The taiga lies in developed countries that have well-established economic systems and scientific networks. This is a good starting point for governments, industrialists, and scientists of different nationalities to work together to find better ways to manage the taiga in a sustainable way.

## The future demand for wood

According to FAO figures for the year 2000, humans consume about 160 billion cubic feet (4.4 billion $m^3$) of wood annually from a global growing stock of 13.7 trillion cubic feet (386 billion $m^3$). Based on the predicted increase in the global human population size, and taking into account the increasing commercialization and industrialization of poorer countries, many analysts estimate that global demand for wood is likely to increase by about 30 percent by the year 2025. To what extent can the taiga contribute to this growing demand?

Russia contains the largest untapped forest acres, and with more than half of its forest area currently inaccessible because of poor transport infrastructure, there is great potential for Russia's forests to help bridge this gap, providing such exploitation is properly managed. Throughout the taiga, it is becoming imperative to crop trees so that every part of the plant is utilized. Already, a wide variety of wood-based composites and other products exist that utilize material previously regarded as waste, such as sawdust, shavings, wood chips, and bark chipping. Undoubtedly, increasing scientific knowledge of how to manage tree stands through cropping, fire management, and disease and pest control will result in greater efficiencies. Breeding programs and genetic engineering can provide tree stock that will grow faster, have better wood qualities for commercial use, and be more disease-, pest-, and fire-resistant.

Ultimately, however, methods of increasing production will need to be complemented by reducing the demand for wood. There is great scope for recycling timber and wood

## Certification

Certification is a tool for encouraging companies to engage in sound, sustainable forestry practice. Providing companies conform to agreed-upon practice, they can market their wood and other forest products with the endorsement of a certifying body. This can improve the marketability of their products in a more environmentally aware consumer market. The Forest Stewardship Council (FSC), founded in 1993, operates internationally and is the most widespread certification scheme operating in boreal forestry. The FSC seeks to promote "environmentally appropriate, socially beneficial, and economically viable management of the world's forests." It does so, in its own words, by "setting a worldwide standard of widely recognized and respected Principles of Forest Management." Wood and forest products produced by FSC-endorsed companies can carry the FSC logo as a "green label."

pulp products. Alternatives to roundwood and lumber as building materials are likely to be found. And crops other than trees can be harvested to produce products with similar properties to those of wood or pulp. For example, sugarcane fibers can be used in place of pulp for some forms of paper manufacture. If all else fails, people will have to get used to living in dwellings that are either smaller or that contain fewer wood products.

## Taiga: carbon sink or carbon source?

Nearly two-thirds of the world's taiga lie in Russia. In recent years, Russian scientists and foresters have suggested that the boreal forest could be managed to increase the rate at which the forest is taking carbon dioxide out of the air. This could be a way of helping to slow down or reverse the buildup of carbon dioxide in the atmosphere. Reducing atmospheric carbon could reduce the enhanced greenhouse effect and help combat global warming.

If Russia's boreal forest is taking more carbon dioxide out of the air than it is adding, then it is acting as a carbon "sink" (an overall absorber of carbon from the atmosphere). But scientists across the world are still unsure whether the world's boreal forest overall is a carbon sink or not (see "Global warming and the taiga," pages 55–58).

In the last few thousand years, boreal forests have probably acted as carbon sinks. They take carbon out of the air and trap it in plant material, and when the plants die, not all the dead matter decays. Much of it becomes trapped as peat, so its carbon is not recycled and returned to the atmosphere. The peat is a rich store of carbon. Only if the peat decomposes or is burnt as a fuel does the trapped carbon return to the atmosphere, predominantly as carbon dioxide.

In the last 30 years, however, boreal regions have been warming slightly, and the areas of permafrost beneath the taiga are probably shrinking as some of the frozen ground melts. When this happens, the ice releases trapped carbon dioxide and methane—both potent greenhouse gases. At the same time, the overlying peat decomposes faster as it warms, producing more carbon dioxide. Under warmer conditions, fires are more likely, and burning wood is another source of carbon dioxide. Overall, the warming boreal forest may be a source (an emitter) of carbon dioxide into the atmosphere.

Much more research will be needed to work out whether Russia's boreal forest is a carbon source or a carbon sink and how the balance might be shifting. There are many factors to take into account. Fires, insect infestations, and logging all reduce the taiga's capacity to absorb carbon dioxide. Working out how much carbon dioxide the forest absorbs over a year is complicated because the living forest absorbs and releases different amounts of carbon dioxide at different times of the year, as does the peat beneath it. The balance also varies from one part of the forest to another. Scientists have to gather vast amounts of data from many sources over several years and then use powerful computer models to predict whether a forest is a carbon source or sink overall. In doing so, scientists will discover which parts of the forest are the best carbon dioxide absorbers, which are the worst emitters, and therefore how the forest might be managed to best absorb carbon dioxide.

Some scientists have suggested that planting more conifers in and around the edges and spaces of the taiga forest would absorb more carbon dioxide and help counter global warming. This could have a small positive effect, but not nearly enough to make much difference. For example, planting conifers at the edges of the taiga would be seeking to grow the trees in conditions that are less than ideal. The trees would not grow as well as normal and would photosynthesize less than the average. In any case, the boundaries of the taiga are changing. International groups of researchers as part of the IPCC estimate that the taiga would have to shift northward by somewhere in the region of two miles (about 3 km) a year over the next century for boreal trees to remain in similar climatic conditions to those they experience today.

Between the 1970s and the 1990s, the average amount of North American boreal forest burned each year more than doubled. Scientific commentators blamed the shift in combustion to a warmer, drier climate. This trend is likely to continue. Fires add carbon dioxide to the air, from the burned trees but also from the top layers of soil that contain partly decayed plant matter.

## Accommodating alternative views of the taiga

As we have seen, the biological nature of the taiga varies from North America to Europe to Asia, but the differences are all variations on a theme. Even though the precise species might vary from region to region, the dominance of conifers, the abundance of peat bogs, the grazing by deer, and the range of birds exploiting similar ways of life are parts of a common theme. But according to Canadian ecologist David Henry, author of *Canada's Boreal Forest,* despite the common biological theme, the way different human societies view the taiga and exploit it varies enormously from one part of the taiga to another.

Many Americans and Canadians regard the taiga as a wilderness of little economic value. This view has a long historical tradition. In 1670, King Charles II of England signed over 3 million square miles (7.7 million km²) of land bordering Hudson Bay to the Hudson Bay Company. He asked for no money in return, apparently glad for someone to take control of this territory. As recently as the late 1980s, several Canadian provinces were happy to sign away forestry rights to foreign-owned corporations, in many cases asking only for royalties (a small percentage of the income) from timber removal plus guarantees that local jobs would be generated. Environmental considerations were seen as relatively less important.

The perception of most traditional taiga peoples is in sharp contrast to the more recent Canadian view of the taiga as a vast, unproductive land. Many traditional taiga peoples view the boreal forest as part of a society to which all physical objects, plants, animals, and people belong. The living and nonliving parts of the environment are seamlessly interconnected.

In modern Sweden, by further contrast, the life of many city-dwellers includes regular visits to the countryside. Families walk and picnic in the woods or cross-country ski in the mountains. The Swedish culture contains many references to traditional folklore involving the natural forest and its inhabitants. According to a popular Swedish saying, a small forest cottage lies at the heart of every Swede. The cottage signifies connection with the land, and many families own a forest cottage that dates back over several generations. Such forest cottages or cabins are a common feature of Scandinavian and Russian cultures, where they come under a variety of names, including *mókki* or *dacha*. This apparent connection with nature and its importance in the culture has not, however, prevented the Swedes from reducing many of their multispecies forest stands to single-species in the last 200 years.

As for Russia, following the revolutions of 1917 and the formation and growth of the USSR, the way the taiga has been exploited has changed. Russian government perceptions of the value of the taiga region have likewise changed. Before 1917, Russia's czars (ruling monarchs) controlled Siberia by giving away large areas to their supporters to manage, among them Cossacks, a Russian cultural group of mixed origin originally noted for their warlike character and skill at horse riding. During the 20th century, Siberia became, on the one hand, linked with gulags (forced labor camps), where those perceived as political threats were sent. On the other hand, Siberia's taiga became the regular savior of Russia's economy. During the 1920s and 1930s, Western governments prevented the sale of many goods and services that would enable the Soviet Union to develop and run modern industries and transport systems. Time and again, the Soviets found valuable resources in Siberia, first in the form of petroleum oil and natural gas, and later in the discovery of precious metals and gems. With the collapse of the Soviet Union in 1991 and the increasing demand for foreign currency to support an ailing economy, parts of the Russian taiga are being exploited in an unsustainable manner to quickly raise cash. Forestry rights have been sold to Japanese-owned companies, and large areas of the southern taiga have been clear-cut, with few attempts to regenerate the forest. Siberia continues to be viewed by many as a land of opportunity where quick money can be made with little concern for environmental damage.

## A local mixed economy

Övertorneå is a rural community in Sweden that is similar in size to a U.S. county. Övertorneå is unusual for a taiga region. It straddles the Arctic Circle yet it is warmed by the North Atlantic Drift, which makes its climate unusually mild. Farmers raise dairy cattle and grow vegetables and cereal crops. In the lowlands of Övertorneå there is a long tradition of farming using organic farming principles—that is, recycling using natural processes without the use of artificial additives such as chemical fertilizers or pesticides. In the highlands, agriculture gives way to reindeer herding and forestry.

By the late 1970s, many young people had left the community to work in towns and cities. In the 1980s, with government support, there was an injection of money and interest in making Övertorneå an ecological community. This is a community with a very mixed economy that seeks to conserve its resources with minimal negative impact on the environment. Young people began to return.

Today Övertorneå supports a rich variety of enterprises that seek to harness natural resources in a sustainable way. Villagers in Svanstein have developed a forestry approach that uses sheep to thin the growth of plants between the trees, rather than using herbicides (weedkillers). The sheep provide wool for local weavers who make traditional, hand-woven garments and cloths dyed with colors extracted from native plants. In the village of Rantajärvi, several families have banded together to set up a heritage center that incorporates a farm. The center has run successfully since the early 1980s, and many youngsters from other parts of Sweden live and work on the farm for a few weeks a year. As part of the experience they learn about the history, culture, and local dialect of the region.

Although Siberia's forests contain among the largest stands of old-growth forest in the world, the World Wildlife Fund (WWF) recently estimated that the existing national parks and protected areas formed an insufficient network for a region of such great ecological importance. The WWF and other nongovernmental organizations, as part of the Taiga Rescue Network (TRN), are pressing for a connected system of wildlife reserves that fully represent the diversity of Siberia's taiga. They are also promoting sustainable forest practices, such as selective logging rather than clear-cutting. By processing timber products locally rather than exporting raw logs, more wealth can be generated to benefit local people. Processing produce locally can also be encouraged for other forest products, such as medicinal plants, berries, and mushrooms. At the same time, wildlife tourism that causes minimal disruption to the local environment is also being developed.

Important lessons can be learned from views of the taiga forest held by traditional peoples. It is a land to be valued, nurtured, and carefully managed. Just as traditional peoples take limited amounts of the taiga's products and exploit different resources with the changing seasons, so modern views of the taiga could incorporate the notion of the taiga offering a very mixed economy. Rather than exploiting the taiga on a massive scale for assets that become exhausted—as in the case of nonrenewable resources such as oil, gas, and mined metals and gems—modern users of the taiga can carefully harvest renewable resources in ways that are sustainable in the longer term.

Many people who live and work in the taiga do so because of the deep satisfaction they gain from a close connection with nature. They may not earn vast amounts of money, but they have a high quality of life and are very self-sufficient. They construct their own buildings, barter goods and services, and work cooperatively with others in the community. This is a far cry from the urban, cash-linked economy that many North Americans, northwest Europeans, and Russians experience.

A strong subsistence economy can flourish in the taiga, but only when it is not compromised by large-scale industries such as mining, timber harvesting, and commercial fishing that are managed without concern for long-term sustainability. The subsistence economy and the cash-rich economy can exist side-by-side, with people earning cash from part-time or full-time work (see sidebar). But to maintain this diversity will probably require less intensive exploitation of the taiga than is currently planned.

Examples do exist that suggest how elements of this mixed economy could be managed. In northern Saskatchewan since the 1970s, farmers have developed an expanding rural industry growing wild rice in slow-moving streams and creeks. Artificial fertilizers are not used, and the enterprise has demonstrated its sustainability. The thousands of small bodies of water in the Canadian taiga could be managed as non-intensive trout farms, with fish feeding on mosquito and other insect larvae that flourish in these waters. Many of the taiga's forest products—ranging from wild honey and berries to herbal remedies—could be sold at premium rates by small concerns.

Already, the Canadian taiga supports a rapidly growing wildlife tourism and environmental education industry. Alongside these ventures run heritage enterprises that seek to convey the lifestyle and land-management concerns of traditional communities. Not only do such activities bring in vital income, but they can also nurture the kinds of values that will help people appreciate and safeguard the taiga.

The world's taiga forests have a value beyond money. Part of the taiga's value lies in the timber it contains, the water in its lakes and rivers, and the fish that swim in them. But it also lies in the forest's capacity to replenish the air, cleanse freshwater, and prevent flooding. The taiga provides a home and income for millions of people. Beyond these benefits, the forests and their communities of plants and animals have a matchless beauty and importance of their own. The northern forests may have a surface simplicity, but the solutions to their continued well-being are not straightforward. In a rapidly changing world, managing the taiga forests will require us to use both ingenuity and wisdom. Current scientific knowledge of the taiga and patterns of forest ownership reveal that management policies and regulations cannot be applied uniformly across this vast expanse of forest. Each area of taiga forest has its own particular blend of circumstances—biological, social, and economic. The key challenge for the 21st century is how to use our scientific knowledge to inform boreal forest management practice at different scales of magnitude, from international to local. Meeting this challenge will help us to act as custodians of these majestic northern forests in ways that are beneficial to ourselves, taiga's wildlife, and the wider biosphere.

# GLOSSARY

**acid rain**   rain made more acidic by oxides of nitrogen and sulfur added to the atmosphere by some forms of air pollution

**alga (plural algae)**   a simple plantlike organism that photosynthesizes

**Algonquian**   a family of Native American languages that originate from eastern Asia. Algonquian languages are spoken by traditional peoples in eastern Canada and the eastern United States

**angiosperm**   a plant belonging to the class Angiospermae. An angiosperm bears flowers and has broad, flat leaves supported by veins

**Arctic Circle**   an imaginary line encircling the Earth at 66°33′N. To the north of this line there is at least 24 hours of continuous daylight in midsummer

**asexual reproduction**   reproduction that does not involve the mixing of genetic material from more than one source

**asthenosphere**   a slowly moving layer within Earth's mantle that causes plates to move

**Athabascan**   a family of Native American languages that are spoken by traditional peoples in western Canada

**atmosphere**   the layer of air enclosing the Earth

**bacterium (plural bacteria)**   a single-celled microorganism that lacks a true nucleus

**basal slip**   the sliding of a glacier along its base

**Bering land bridge (Beringia)**   the Bering Strait, lying between Asia and North America, drained of seawater. The Bering land bridge has probably formed at least three times in the last 70,000 years

**biodiversity (biological diversity)**   the variety of life-forms in a locality

**biomass**   the total mass of life-forms in a locality

**biome**   a major ecological division of the living world. A biome is distinguished by its climate, soil, and wildlife. Taiga, tundra, and desert are examples

**bog**   a type of wetland in which partly decayed plant matter, especially sphagnum moss, builds up to form a thick layer of peat

**boreal forest**   an alternative name for taiga forest. It is the northern, conifer-rich forest that grows densely between latitudes 45°N and 65°N

**broad-leaved tree**   a tree belonging to the class Angiospermae. It bears flowers and has broad, flat leaves distinct from the needle leaves of conifers

**canopy**   the layer at the top of a forest containing leaves and branches

**carbon dioxide**   a major gas released when carbon-rich substances, such as fossil fuels, burn in air. It is also released by respiring organisms. Carbon dioxide is a greenhouse gas and is believed to be a major contributor to global warming

**clear-cutting (clear-felling)**   the process of cutting down almost all trees in a given area irrespective of their age or size

**climate**   the typical pattern of weather in a place over many years

**climax community**   the biological community that develops at the end of an ecological succession, provided local conditions do not undergo major disturbance

**commensalism**   a close relationship between two organisms of different species in which one (the commensal) benefits and the other (the host) neither benefits nor is harmed

**cone**   a structure containing the sexually reproductive parts of a conifer

**conifer**   a tree or shrub that bears cones

**convection current**   the vertical circulation of a gas or liquid due to warm regions rising and cool regions sinking

**consumer**   an organism such as an animal or fungus that consumes other organisms or organic matter derived from them

**Coriolis effect**   the apparent deflection of winds and ocean currents caused by Earth's rotation. It causes anticyclones (high-pressure systems) and mid-latitude oceanic gyres to rotate in a clockwise direction in the Northern Hemisphere

**crust**   the solid, rocky outer layer of the Earth on which the land and sea lie

**deciduous**   plants that typically shed their leaves each year

**decomposer**   an organism, especially a bacterium or fungus, that assists in the decay of organic matter from once-living organisms

**dormant** so inactive as to appear lifeless. Most seeds remain dormant until they germinate

**earthquake** shaking of the Earth's crust usually caused by volcanoes or Earth's plates grinding against one another

**ecological succession** the development of an ecosystem in a distinct series of stages, in which the biological community at one stage produces conditions suitable for the development of the next

**ecosystem** the system comprising the community of organisms and its habitat found in a particular locality

**ecotone** the edge of a biome; where one biome merges into another

**epiphyte** a plant that grows on the surface of another plant but does not obtain nutrients from it

**erosion** the breakdown and removal of rock or soil by the action of wind, temperature change, or moving water or ice

**evaporation** the conversion of a liquid to a gas

**evergreen** a plant that keeps its leaves year-round. Most conifers are evergreens

**fertile** capable of sustaining plant growth

**food chain** a simple sequence showing which organism feeds on another organism within a community

**food web** the interconnections between food chains within a community

**forest stand** a community of trees, plus associated organisms, sufficiently uniform in age and species composition to be managed as a unit

**fragmentation** the breakup of a connected ecosystem, such as a forest, into separate patches

**frost heave** the lifting and mixing of soil produced by expanding and then thawing pockets of ice

**fungus (plural fungi)** an organism, neither plant nor animal, with a complex cell structure that obtains its food ready-made. Fungi include mushrooms, toadstools, and yeasts

**genetics** the scientific study of how an organism's characteristics are inherited and expressed

**glacier** a mass of snow and ice flowing slowly downhill

**global warming** a sustained rise in average surface temperatures across the world

**greenhouse effect** the warming effect caused by greenhouse gases in the atmosphere, such as carbon dioxide, trapping some of the infrared radiation emitted from Earth's surface

**habitat**   the place where a specific organism, or a community of organisms, lives

**herbaceous**   having a nonwoody stem, as in the case of a common wood sorrel or an orchid plant

**hibernation**   for some animals, a period of dormancy in winter when body functions drop far below normal

**humus**   partly decayed animal and plant matter in soil. It typically forms as a dark surface layer on soil

**hypha (plural hyphae)**   the feeding tube of a fungus

**ice age (glacial period or glaciation)**   a cold period in Earth's history lasting thousands of years when glaciers and ice sheets are more extensive than usual and sea levels are lower. The most recent ice age ended about 12,000 years ago

**ice sheet**   an extensive, thick layer of ice covering a major landmass. Ice sheets cover most of Antarctica and Greenland

**invertebrate**   an animal without a backbone (vertebral column)

**ion**   an atom or molecule with an overall positive or negative electrical charge

**latitude**   a measure of angular distance north or south of the equator. The equator lies at zero degrees latitude, the North Pole at 90°N, and the South Pole at 90°S

**lava**   molten rock (magma) on Earth's surface

**leaching**   the depletion of soluble substances from the upper soil by downward-percolating water

**lichen**   a type of organism formed as a dependent beneficial partnership between an alga and a fungus

**limestone**   sedimentary rock containing mostly calcium carbonate. Chalk is an example

**lithosphere**   the outer rocky layer of the Earth comprising the crust and upper part of the mantle. About 20 plates make up the lithosphere

**loess**   dusty deposits of windblown silt and clay

**longitude**   a measure of angular distance east or west of the Greenwich Meridian at zero degrees longitude (an imaginary line passing north-south through Greenwich, London). The International Date Line lies at 180° longitude

**magma**   molten rock beneath Earth's surface

**mammal**   a warm-blooded, hairy animal that feeds its young with milk

**mantle**   the layer of dense, hot rock lying between Earth's crust and core

**migration**   the mass movement of animals from one region to another, usually to find food or a breeding place

**mixed economy**   the wealth and resources of a community managed in such a way that there is a mix of cash-rich and subsistence activities

**mixed forest**   forest that contains a mix of conifer and broad-leaved trees

**moraine**   a deposit of material left at the edge of a glacier or ice sheet

**mutation**   a sudden alteration in the normal complement of genetic material. It occurs most commonly at cell division

**mutualism**   a close relationship between two organisms of different species in which both benefit

**mycorrhiza (plural mycorrhizae)**   a close association (symbiosis) between a soil fungus and a plant in which both benefit. The term means "fungus-root"

**nutrients**   substances, such as nitrates and phosphates, that plants need in small amounts to make organic (carbon-based) substances by photosynthesis

**old-growth forest**   a forest largely undisturbed by human activity for many decades. It contains a high proportion of old trees

**outwash**   sediment deposited by the streams from a glacier or ice sheet

**oxygen**   a gas in the air that most animals and plants require for respiration

**ozone**   a substance that forms in the stratosphere when oxygen absorbs ultraviolet radiation

**Paleolithic**   having to do with the old stone age, when ancient cultures constructed simple stone implements

**paleontology**   the scientific study and interpretation of fossils

**parasitism**   a close relationship between two organisms of different species in which one (the parasite) obtains benefit from the other (the host), usually in the form of nutrition. The host is harmed, although the effect may be slight

**peat**   partly decayed plant matter that builds up in marshy ground in cold or temperate climates. In bogs, peat is mostly formed of partly decayed sphagnum moss

**permafrost**   ground that is permanently frozen beneath the surface. In practice, this means rock or soil that has been shown to be frozen throughout the year

**photosynthesis**   the process by which plants, and some protists and bacteria, trap sunlight to make organic (carbon-rich) substances such as carbohydrates

**plastic flow**   gradual movement between particles of a solid (such as ice crystals within a glacier) without fracturing

**plate (tectonic or lithospheric plate)**   a segment of Earth's rocky surface consisting of crust and attached upper mantle. About 20 slowly moving plates make up Earth's surface

**plate tectonics**   the modern theory that the Earth's surface is divided into plates. Their movements generate continental drift and are responsible for phenomena such as earthquakes and volcanoes close to plate boundaries

**podzol**   a common soil of cold regions where precipitation is high and evaporation low. The soil has an ash-colored layer near the surface from which metals and clay have been washed. Deeper, it contains an orange-brown layer where some of these substances have accumulated

**polar**   referring to Earth's poles or the nearby regions

**pollen**   dustlike powder produced in cones and flowers. It contains male gametes

**pollination**   transfer of pollen from male to female parts of cones or flowers

**pollution**   release of physical or chemical agents into the environment that potentially cause harm

**precipitation**   water in the atmosphere that falls to Earth's surface as rain, hail, sleet, or snow, or settles as dew

**predator**   an animal of one species that kills and eats individuals of another animal species (its prey)

**primary succession**   a series of plant communities, one replacing another, beginning with a surface devoid of vegetation

**producer**   an organism in the community that makes food by manufacturing organic substances from simple inorganic ones. In a forest ecosystem, the major producers are photosynthetic plants

**rain shadow**   a region where rainfall is low because nearby mountains block the arrival of rain-bearing clouds

**respiration**   the process inside cells by which organisms break down food molecules to release energy

**secondary succession**   a series of plant communities, one replacing another, beginning with the destruction of part or all of the existing vegetation

**seed-tree method**   a tree-harvesting method in which most mature trees are cut down but some are left standing to provide seed for growth of the replacement stand

**selective cutting**   a tree-harvesting method in which a few selected trees are cut down but many others are left standing. This method works well for regrowth of shade-loving trees in mixed conifer and broad-leaved forests

**sexual reproduction** reproduction that involves the mixing of genetic material from more than one source

**shelterwood method** a tree-harvesting method in which some mature trees are cut down but others are left standing to provide seed and shade for growth of the replacement stand

**shrub** a woody plant, smaller than a tree, which usually has several stems.

**silviculture** the planting, tending, and harvesting of trees

**species** the world population of similar-looking individuals that interbreed to produce fertile offspring

**sphagnum moss** the most common type of moss found in bogs. It can hold unusually large amounts of water

**stratosphere** the part of the atmosphere immediately above the lower atmosphere (troposphere). It contains the ozone layer

**striation** in geology, a scratch or groove in bedrock created by sediment in a moving glacier

**strip cutting** a modified form of clear-cutting in which a narrow strip of forest is cleared. Establishment of trees in the clear-cut strip benefits from the presence of unharvested trees nearby

**subsistence economy** an economy based on families producing goods primarily for themselves, with little left over to barter or sell

**symbiosis** a close relationship between two individuals of different species in which one or both benefit

**taiga** the conifer-dominated forest biome, with associated lakes, rivers, and wetlands, found between latitudes 45° and 70°N

**temperate** referring to the regions of the globe that have moderate, seasonal climates. They lie between about latitudes 40° and 60°

**trade winds** prevailing winds that blow toward the equator

**tree** a large, woody plant usually with a single stem, called the trunk

**trophic level** the energy level in a food chain or food web. Organisms at the first trophic level are producers. Organisms at higher trophic levels are consumers

**troposphere** the lower layer of the atmosphere. It contains Earth's weather systems

**tundra** treeless plains of mosses, lichens, shrubs, and grasses that lie to the north of the taiga

**ultraviolet (UV) radiation** electromagnetic radiation of wavelengths just beyond the violet end of the visible spectrum. In high doses, UV radiation can be harmful to life

**vascular**   having specialized vessels for circulating fluids

**vertebrate**   an animal with a backbone (vertebral column). Fishes, amphibians, reptiles, birds, and mammals are vertebrates

**volcano**   a place on Earth's surface from which lava erupts

**water vapor**   water in the form of a gas

**weather**   the state of the lower atmosphere at a given place and time in terms of factors such as air pressure, cloudiness, humidity, precipitation, temperature, and wind strength

**wetland**   a low-lying area of land that is water covered or has water-saturated soil

**wood product**   a product derived from a forest's harvested wood. Wood products include fuelwood, roundwood, lumber, wood composites, and paper

# FURTHER READING

Barnes, Burton V., Donald R. Zak, Shirley R. Denton, and Stephen H. Spurr. *Forest Ecology.* 4th ed. New York: John Wiley & Sons, 1998.

Bastedo, James. *Reaching North: A Celebration of the Subarctic.* Red Deer, Alberta: Red Deer College Press, 1998.

Brownson, J. M. Jamil. *In Cold Margins.* Missoula, Mont.: Northern Rim Press, 1995.

Canadian Geographic. *The Boreal Forest: The National Atlas of Canada.* Ottawa: Canadian Geographic, 1996.

Edmonds, Robert L., James K. Agee, and Robert I. Gara. *Forest Health and Protection.* Boston: McGraw-Hill, 2000.

Food and Agriculture Organization of the United Nations. *State of the World's Forests: 2003.* Rome: Food and Agriculture Organization of the United Nations, 2003.

Gawthrop, Daniel. *Vanishing Halo: Saving the Boreal Forest.* Vancouver: Greystone Books, Douglas and MacIntyre, 1999.

Henry, J. David. *Canada's Boreal Forest.* Washington, D.C.: Smithsonian Institution Press, 2002.

Karnosky, D. F., K. E. Percy, A. H. Chappelka, C. Simpson, and J. Pikkarainen, eds. *Air Pollution, Global Change, and Forests in the New Millennium.* Amsterdam: Elsevier, 2003.

Kellomäki, Seppo. *Forest Resources and Sustainable Management.* Helsinki, Finland: Fapet Oy, 1998.

Lanken, Dane. "Boreal Forest." *Canadian Geographic,* May/June 1996, 26–33.

Lynch, Wayne. *The Great Northern Kingdom: Life in the Boreal Forest.* Markham, Canada: Fitzhenry and Whiteside, 2001.

Maybank, Blake, and Peter Mertz. *The National Parks and Other Wild Places of Canada.* London: New Holland, 2001.

Nyland, Ralph D. *Silviculture: Concepts and Applications.* 2nd ed. New York: McGraw-Hill, 2002.

Smith, David M., Bruce C. Larson, Matthew J. Kelty, and P. Mark S. Ashton. *The Practice of Silviculture: Applied Forest Ecology.* New York: John Wiley & Sons, 1997.

Watson, Robert T., Ian R. Noble, Bert Bolin, N. H. Ravindranath, David J. Verardo, and David J. Dokken, eds. *Land Use, Land-Use Change, and Forestry.* Cambridge: Intergovernmental Panel on Climate Change/Cambridge University Press, 2003.

Woodward, Susan L. *Biomes of Earth: Terrestrial, Aquatic, and Human-Dominated.* Westport, Conn.: Greenwood Press, 2003.

Worldwatch Institute, ed. *Vital Signs 2003: The Trends That Are Shaping Our Future.* New York: W. W. Norton, 2003.

# WEB SITES

**American Association for the Advancement of Science**

URL: http://www.aaas.org

An international nonprofit organization dedicated to advancing science around the world.

**Boreal Forest Network**

URL: http://www.borealnet.org

The North American affiliate of the Taiga Rescue Network, an international nongovernmental organization that seeks to restore and protect boreal forest.

**Canadian Boreal Initiative**

URL: http://www.borealcanada.ca

An independent organization working with conservationists, taiga peoples, and industry to link science, policy, and conservation activities in Canada's boreal region.

**Canadian Forests**

URL: http://www.canadian-forests.com

A web site that acts as a portal to other web sites that represent organizations with interests in Canada's forests and its forestry.

**Canadian Institute of Forestry**

URL: http://www.cif-ifc.org

The professional organization representing Canada's forest practitioners in government, industry, research, education, and consulting.

### FAO Forestry Department

URL: http://www.fao.org/forestry

The Forestry Department of the Food and Agriculture Organization (FAO) of the United Nations.

### Forest.ru

URL: http://www.forest.ru

The web site platform for Russia's nongovernmental organizations that have particular interest in boreal forest.

### National Aeronautics and Space Administration's (NASA) earth science pages

URL: http://www.nasa.gov/topics/earth

NASA's web pages that include information on weather, climate, and pollution, including that of relevance to the taiga region.

### National Oceanic and Atmospheric Administration's (NOAA) climate pages

URL: http://www.noaa.gov/climate.html

NOAA's web pages include information on weather, climate, and pollution, including that of relevance to the taiga region.

### Parks Canada

URL: http://www.parkscanada.pch.gc.ca/agen/index_e.asp

The agency with a remit to protect Canada's national parks and to foster public understanding, appreciation, and enjoyment of them.

### Taiga Rescue Network

URL: http://www.taigarescue.org

The international network with more than 150 nongovernmental member organizations that are committed to sensitive, sustainable development of the boreal forest.

## The World Conservation Union (IUCN)

URL: http://www.iucn.org

The world's largest organization that works closely with governments and international agencies to foster wildlife conservation alongside sustainable development.

## United Nations Environment Program (UNEP)

URL: http://www.unep.org

The United Nations agency with an environmental focus on conservation and sustainable development.

## UNEP World Conservation Monitoring Center (UNEP-WCMC)

URL: http://www.unep-wcmc.org

UNEP-WCMC compiles and publishes data on the state of the world's biodiversity.

## UNESCO's Man and the Biosphere (MAB) program

URL: http://www.unesco.org/mab/about.htm

The United Nations Educational, Scientific and Cultural Organization's web site that relates to the MAB program. It includes information on the world's biosphere reserves.

## World Resources Institute (WRI)

URL: http://www.wri.org

An independent, nonprofit environmental research and policy organization based in Washington, D.C.

## WWF (formerly, the World Wildlife Fund)

URL: http://www.panda.org

An international nongovernmental organization that carries out promotional and practical conservation work in many countries, including field projects and scientific research.

Note: *Italic* page numbers refer to illustrations.